An Introduction
to Therapeutic Communities

Therapeutic Communities
Series editors: Rex Haigh & Jan Lees

The Therapeutic Community movement holds a multidisciplinary view of health which is bassed on ideas of collective responsibility, citizenship and empowerment. The tradition has a long and distinguished history and is experiencing a revival of interest in contemporary theory and practice. It draws from many different principles - including analytic, behavioural, creative , educational and humanistic – in the framework of a group-based view of the social origins and maintenance of much overwhelming distress, mental ill-health and deviant behaviour. Therapeutic Community principles are applicable in a wide variety of settings, and this series will reflect that.

Therapeutic Communities: Past, Present and Future
Therapeutic Communities 2
Edited by Rex Haigh and Penelope Campling
ISBN 1 85302 614 X hb
ISBN 1 85302 615 8 pb

An Introduction
to Therapeutic Communities
David Kennard

Therapeutic Communities 1

Jessica Kingsley Publishers
London and Philadelphia

First published in 1983 by Routledge.

This completely revised and updated 2nd edition first published in the United Kingdom in 1998 by

Jessica Kingsley Publishers Ltd,
116 Pentonville Road,
London N1 9JB,
England

and

325 Chestnut Street,
Philadelphia, PA 19106, USA.

www.jkp.com

Copyright © 1998 David Kennard
Chapter 12 Copyright © 1998 Jeff Roberts

Library of Congress Cataloging in Publication Data

A CIP catalogue record for this book is available from the Library of Congress

British Library Cataloguing in Publication Data

Kennard, David

Introduction to therapeutic communities. - (Therapeutic communities ; 1)

1. Therapeutic communities

I. Title

362.2'0425

ISBN 1-85302-603-4

Printed and Bound in Great Britain by
Athenaeum Press, Gateshead, Tyne and Wear

Contents

Part II: Working in a therapeutic community

Part III: Further information

To my mother, otherwise known as Celia of Harrow,
and in memory of my father Jack Kennard

Preface

It seemed a fairly light job at first, revising this book for its second edition. Then I began to go through each chapter and realized just how much had changed in the fifteen years since it was first published. In 1983 most therapeutic communities were based in hospitals. Now few are, and those that are have become far more focused – for example on people with what are termed severe personality disorders. New therapeutic communities are being created in the voluntary sector – small, autonomous organizations with dedicated staff and the freedom to innovate – and in the prison system. Chapter 4 in the first edition has been expanded to two chapters – Chapters 5 and 6 – to do justice to these developments.

Another change has been the general sense of how much more educated the field is now. When I wrote the first edition I tried very hard to use simple straightforward language, avoiding more theoretical or technical terms (my role models were Alistair Cook and Mary Goldring). I was mindful that many readers would be unfamiliar with theories relating to therapeutic communities, and might be uncomfortable with any kind of academic writing. Today this seems less likely. The increasing numbers of people going though higher education, National Vocational Qualifications and schemes for accrediting experiential learning, together with the increasing demarcation of different therapeutic models, all suggest that the aspiring therapeutic community worker of today is likely to be better informed, and to demand a better informed text, than would have been the case fifteen years ago. (I am writing here about the scene in the United Kingdom but I think similar changes have gone on in other countries too.) In revising the book I have no longer pursued the holy grail of simplicity. This may have resulted in a less readable or approachable book, and where that is so I apologize. On the other hand I hope it has allowed me to provide a more authoritative text which can act as a resource and pointer to the many developments that have taken place in therapeutic community work. Being editor of the journal *Therapeutic Communities* for the past seven years has given me a unique opportunity to be aware of new ideas and new projects both in the UK and abroad, through the papers sent in for publication. I have tried where possible to make use of this awareness and to share with the reader those developments that have impressed or excited me.

The times *are* exciting for therapeutic communities. From being put out to graze in the 1970s, and being cold-shouldered by the NHS in the 1980s, there are many signs that they are now coming to be recognized as a valid and effective form of treatment. At the time of writing, plans are in place to create two more Henderson-style units in order to give national access to this particular model, and to build a second prison along the lines of HMP Grendon; while the psychiatric establishment is looking to therapeutic community expertise for help in developing a skilful and informed Community Psychiatry. In the voluntary sector where many severely and long-term mentally ill people now receive support – in residential and day care projects – the therapeutic community offers a model of humane containment, combined with a sustainable staff/resident learning environment that makes it more attractive than models based purely on skills acquisition or normalization.

A further sign of the changing times is that it no longer seems necessary to try to provide an information section listing every kind of national and local organization that might be worth contacting for further information. Things are better organized now. A few key addresses will take you where you want to go. I have also dropped the attempt to summarize in chart form the characteristics of different kinds of therapeutic communities. This kind of exercise appeals at a certain stage in one's life, but I have the impression that for all the work involved it is of little practical use and is not much noticed except by other chart makers.

Amid the changes some things remain constant. In the Preface to the first edition I wrote about the 'therapeutic community impulse' as a desire 'to focus on the quality of relationships and communication between people, on the way they naturally set about dealing with one another, as the essential working material of treatment'. I believe this still to be true and at the heart of the therapeutic community endeavour. The idea of the therapeutic community impulse has since been amplified elsewhere (Kennard 1992), and Hinshelwood (1996) has linked it to the importance of finding 'new ways to restore a bridge across our divisions' – being able to contain the splits that push people into false opposition between partially true answers. This is never easy. The urge for certainty, and the anxiety associated with responsibility for difficult clinical or management decisions, will often tend to push us into treating others as the objects of our efforts to control or manage them. I hope that this book will support that other impulse, to see the fellow human being in the other person, whether client or colleague, and to create environments where everyone can learn to see one another in this way.

York, April 1998

Preface to the First Edition

Something which I am tempted to call the 'therapeutic community impulse' flows through many forms of institutional care, or rather, the people who create them. I mean institution in the sense of any place where people live together (or come together daily) because they can no longer manage to live in their usual family or social environment or are no longer wanted there. These include special schools, psychiatric hospitals, prisons, hostels, day centres. The impulse is difficult to define. It expresses itself in a number of attitudes: liberalism, egalitarianism, psychological mindedness, toleration of the expression of conflicting ideas and a kind of shirt-sleeves informality about the business of helping people. It is an impulse to focus on the quality of relationships and communication between people, on the way they naturally set about dealing with one another, as the essential working material of treatment. This impulse contrasts with others – for example the impulse to make people as uniform and easy to manage as possible, which is found in many institutions as well as in more repressive societies. Or the impulse to look after people in a protective but controlling way which is characteristic of many good hospitals.

I am inclined to believe that these impulses are aspects of human nature and are thus all present, to a greater or lesser extent, in the ways that people have tried to help one another at different times and in different places. The therapeutic community impulse has appeared more or less strongly in different specialities, in different countries, and in different periods of history.

Sometimes it has been accompanied by conscientious thoughtfulness and produced long-lived and well-researched communities; at other times by enthusiastic but naive dogmatism, producing short-lived or Messianic communities. At various times it has been linked to different theories of interpersonal relations. The Christian belief that love will eventually elicit the good in even the worst offender guided many early leaders of therapeutic communities. Later pioneers were more likely to be guided by Freud's theories of unconscious forces pushing people into repetitions of unhappy relationships, for which the cure was understanding rather than love alone. More recently many therapeutic communities have been influenced by those theories broadly labelled as 'humanistic-existential', which emphasize the responsibility each of us has for deciding what kind of person we want to be.

In its various forms and with its changing travelling companions, the therapeutic community impulse has continued to express itself in a wide variety of caring establishments. In this book I have tried to document some of the main forms this expression has taken.

I have written this book primarily for students and trainees in the helping professions who may spend some time in a therapeutic community or come across the idea and want to know more about it. It is also for those who have recently begun to work in a helping community of one sort or another, or are considering whether to do so. A further aim of the book is to introduce therapeutic communities to one another. People who work in one kind of community often know little of what goes on in others, and I hope this book will help to correct a few misconceptions and enable practitioners to feel more informed about each other's approach. Finally I hope it will be useful to anyone who is interested to find out what therapeutic communities are, how they came about, and the ideas and skills relevant to them.

There are three parts. The first provides a detailed description of the way different kinds of therapeutic communities have evolved. This begins with a chapter bringing together the features they share in common – something I want to emphasize, which is why it starts the book. Chapters 2–4 chart the history of therapeutic communities from the era of moral treatment in the eighteenth and nineteenth centuries, through work with maladjusted children in the first part of the twentieth century, and on to experiments in social psychiatry in World War II. Chapters 5–8 then describe the four main kinds of therapeutic community in current use in terms of their history, ideas and practice. Chapter 9 anticipates what the future contributions of therapeutic communities may be. Research findings have not been dealt with as a separate topic but incorporated at relevant points.

The second part is addressed specifically to those readers who are concerned about the experience and practicalities of working in a therapeutic community. Chapter 10 presents an imaginary 'first day' which will bring the material in Part I to life for readers who have not actually been in a therapeutic community, and may help those who have to recognize some of the responses of a newcomer. Chapter 11 offers some practical guidelines for staff and for beginners, and Chapter 12 discusses questions related to the needs and resources for training in therapeutic community work. The final part of the book is a compilation of useful information for finding out more about therapeutic communities.

In writing an introductory book covering different types of therapeutic communities, there is a risk – a likelihood – that my own experience and point of view have influenced the way things are presented. While I have tried to give an accurate picture of each approach, inevitably there is personal judgement, not least about what to include and what to leave out. It may help the reader to be aware of the framework within which the book was put together, if I say what my own interests and experience have been. My interest in therapeutic communities goes back a long way to the mid-1960s. This was the heyday of anti-psychiatry, and as a recent psychology graduate I was drawn to the writings of Ronald Laing and other existential psychotherapists. I visited Kingsley Hall (see Chapter 8) two or three times and became interested in trying to understand mental illness. This led to an interest in mental hospitals and what went on inside them. I worked briefly as a psychiatric nursing assistant and then decided to take a job as a probationer clinical psychologist. While training I became interested in social and interpersonal aspects of psychiatry and found a natural liking for working in groups. A visit to the Henderson Hospital impressed me, and on qualifying in 1970 I moved to Littlemore Hospital in Oxford, where I worked until 1982. There I was able to become involved in two different therapeutic communities. One was a psychiatric admission unit, the other was a new unit for drug abusers which evolved into a self-help therapeutic community partly staffed by former drug addicts. This side-by-side experience prompted several attempts to conceptualize the differences between the two which, looking back, were the beginnings of this book. In addition I became increasingly involved in the activities of the Association of Therapeutic Communities, and through this visited many other communities.

Two experiences had a particular influence on my approach to writing this book. Research projects, which I carried out in the above two communities in collaboration with Robert Clemmey and Steve Wilson, taught me a lot about ordering information, thinking through conceptual problems, and trying to stay within the evidence when making statements. Although this is not a book about research, the discipline of writing it has been similar. The other experience has been my training as a group analyst. Being a patient in an analytic group and participating in a group-analytic climate of supervision and discussion created a perspective which links at a deep level the individual's experience with the way people feel and act in groups and communities. This is a perspective which makes therapeutic communities – and other institutions – fascinating places to work in and think about.

Oxford, October 1982
updated April 1998

Acknowledgements

I am grateful to Annie Borthwick for her valuable comments on Chapter 2 on Quaker values and moral treatment, and to Peter Agulnik who provided me with an up-to-date view of the Ley Community and some of the issues addressed in Chapter 7 on concept-based therapeutic communities. I am indebted to Eric Cullen and his colleagues for publishing *Therapeutic Communities for Offenders* (Wiley 1997) just ahead of this revision which provided a useful source of information for Chapter 5 on personality disorders and Chapter 7, and to Doug Lipton for sending me several of his papers on work in the United States.

The main work of updating Chapter 12 on training, which was written by us jointly in the first edition, has been carried by Jeff Roberts and he wishes it made clear that the opinions expressed in it are his own.

Acknowledgements to the First Edition

The following people made valuable comments on various parts of the book: Liz Burrows, Brian Donellan, George Dunne, Joanne Evans, Heinz Fischer, Bob Hinshelwood, Margaret Howarth, Carolyn Lawson, Liz Smith, Caroline Trimnell and Sue Vogt.

I am grateful to the staff and residents of the following therapeutic communities for allowing me to visit and discussing with me their views and impressions: Arbours Crisis Centre, Ascot Farm, Church Lane Community, Cotswold Community, Henderson Hospital, Ingrebourne Centre, Rutland House, St Charles House.

In particular I am grateful to my colleagues in the Phoenix Unit and Ley Community. The constant interplay of feelings and ideas in these communities has been the testing ground against which the ideas for this book have gradually taken shape. To Peter Agulnik, John McCabe and Bertram Mandelbrote I feel a special debt for the stimulation of their ideas and working approach.

Many friends and colleagues in the Association of Therapeutic Communities have provided inspiration in our formal and informal get-togethers, and to them I should like to express my gratitude.

Tom Main kindly gave permission to quote at length from his lecture, 'The concept of the therapeutic community: Variations and vicissitudes', which first appeared in *Group Analysis* as a supplement to Vol. 10 (2), 1977 and was reprinted in *The Evolution of Group Analysis,* edited by Malcolm Pines in 1983 and published by Routledge.

Finally I should like to thank Verlaine Bowden, who typed and retyped the many drafts through which the book has passed, with interest and good humour.

PART I

The Development
of Therapeutic Communities

CHAPTER 1

Different Origins – Common Attributes

People have used the phrase 'a therapeutic community' to describe quite different sorts of places since the term was first invented in 1946. Since no one has a copyright on it some confusion cannot be avoided, and that is not altogether a bad thing. Limiting the term to one particular type of community could do more harm than good, inhibiting new developments or 'outlawing' certain types of community which might be just as therapeutic as those within the definition. Yet despite their different origins and ways of working, organizations which are known as therapeutic communities do have a number of significant features in common. What I shall try to do in this chapter is first to set out the main different ways in which the term has been used, and then to describe the characteristics which I believe most of these settings have in common.

DIFFERENT ORIGINS

In the early years of therapeutic communities – the 1950s and 1960s – any institution that was trying to improve the lot of its residents could and often did call itself a therapeutic community. This usually meant that it was offering them opportunities for productive, responsible work, for developing their interests and talents and for participating in the day-to-day running of the institution. The term was often used in this way when the place in question had previously been considered decidedly untherapeutic. Mental hospitals called themselves therapeutic communities to signal the new leaf they had turned over in bringing patients normal, decent living conditions, and creating a more humane, stimulating atmosphere. Today the use of the term in this general way has largely disappeared. This is partly because many of the hospitals themselves have closed during the past fifteen years and partly because the more specific uses of the term have become more well known, though not necessarily better understood.

Used in a specific way, the term therapeutic community refers to a particular set of principles and methods used to help people with particular kinds of problems or disorders. This brings us to an unusual source of confusion. By what appears to be historical coincidence the same term was introduced in-dependently in England and the United States, twelve years apart but nonetheless, as far as one can tell, quite independently. In England, psychia-trist and psychoanalyst Tom Main first wrote about therapeutic communi-ties in 1946. At that time he was using the term mainly in the general sense described above, but over the decade that followed there emerged a distinc-tive therapeutic community method largely associated with the work of Maxwell Jones at the Henderson Hospital. David Clark called this 'therape-utic community proper', to distinguish it from the general 'approach' (Clark 1965). It had as its hallmark the democratic sharing of power by all mem-bers of the community – staff and patients alike – in decisions that affected not only the running of the community but also the treatment of the patients. Patients became auxiliary therapists and official hierarchies were reduced as far as possible. More will be said about this kind of therapeutic community later. At this point enough has been said to contrast it with what emerged, 6000 miles away in California, in 1958.

There, a man named Charles Dederich, an ex-alcoholic who had become an ardent member of Alcoholics Anonymous but was dissatisfied with some of its limitations, founded an organization called Synanon where ex-alcoholics and ex-drug addicts could live together and help one another to stay 'clean', i.e. drug-free. The basic principle was a 'no-holds-barred' honest confrontation about anything and everything. Emotional defences or 'cop-outs' were demolished in verbally aggressive encounter groups known as the 'Synanon Game'. The atmosphere was one of righteous, some might say religious, zeal.

Apart from this difference of general tone from the English communities, there were two other major differences. One was that Synanon and many of the communities that followed in its footsteps were run by non-pro-fessionals, run in fact by ex-addicts for ex-addicts. Professionals such as psy-chiatrists and psychologists were distrusted or seen as having little to offer. The second difference was the hierarchical structure that Synanon devel-oped. Ironically, while doctors and nurses in many English mental hospitals were busy dismantling their authority, sharing decisions with patients and striving towards greater informality and equality, ex-addicts in Synanon and elsewhere were busy creating a steeply graded staff and resident hierarchy where decisions were made at the top and obeyed at the bottom, and failure at either end meant confrontation in the encounter group that night. And all in the name of the therapeutic community!

More will be said later about the philosophy and practice of these two types of therapeutic community, but at this point it seems that we really should ask the question, do they have anything in common other than the

name, and the broad aim of helping people? I think the answer to this is undoubtedly yes. Most of the ingredients are the same, only organized in a different way – but this is not the view taken by all therapeutic community
workers. In fact people who work in one or other of these two types of therapeutic community have until recently known little of each other's existence
– indeed the ex-addict communities have generally appeared to ignore the
existence of any other kind of therapeutic community, while leaders of psychiatric therapeutic communities have in the past sought to distance themselves from their American namesakes. 'They are communities and they are
therapeutic, but they do not pretend to be therapeutic communities as described by Maxwell Jones' (Clark 1977). More recently, communications
and mutual acceptance have begun to improve through a recognition of
shared interests in work with young offenders in prisons. In the past twenty
years prisons in Britain, Germany and North America have all developed
therapeutic communities, although those in America are still largely focused
on drug users (Cullen *et al.* 1997).

At the beginning of this chapter I pointed out that no one has a copyright
on the concept of a therapeutic community, and others have used it who are
followers of neither Main, Jones or Dederich. They too have sought to har-
ness the energies present in a small, close community, usually one that shares
a communal household, for the express purpose of helping some or all of its
members to overcome or cope with their personal inadequacies or distress.
Many of these have been inspired by Christian beliefs and values. Two organizations for mentally handicapped people have grown to become international movements: the Camphill Village Communities based on the ideas
of the philosopher and educationalist Rudolf Steiner, and L'Arche communities founded in France by Jean Vanier, while the Richmond Fellowship,
founded by Elly Jansen, has developed into an international network of
houses for people with psychiatric disabilities. There are also those communities offering a direct alternative to mental hospital for people experiencing
a psychotic disturbance; these were inspired by the anti-psychiatry movement of the 1960s, associated with the work of Ronald Laing and David
Cooper.

To summarize so far: there are four broad but distinct ways in which the
term therapeutic community is used.

Therapeutic Community Approach

The transformation of large, asylum-type institutions, especially containers for
the chronically mentally ill, into more active, humane, caring institutions where
the human rights and dignity of the inmates are recognized and respected. Such
organizations are still clearly run by the staff, but their task changes from being

custodians to creating an atmosphere in which residents are trusted and encouraged to take responsibility and initiative. This use of the term is largely confined to the past, although may still be relevant where mental health provisions are at an early stage of development.

Therapeutic Community Proper

The development of small, cohesive communities where therapeutic decisions and functions are shared by the whole community, and where the status differences between staff and resident are greatly reduced though not abandoned. In the field of psychiatry such therapeutic communities are sometimes referred to as the Maxwell Jones or democratic type. In Great Britain the term therapeutic community, when used to describe a small establishment in the domain of mental health, social services, the prison system or provisions for children and adolescents, usually refers to an enterprise of this type. They most frequently deal with problems of severe or borderline personality disorder or social maladjustment.

Concept-Based Therapeutic Community

The development of small, cohesive communities in which the staff and residents form a continuous hierarchy or chain of command. Staff are often qualified for their work by virtue of having been residents in such a community themselves. The names Synanon, Daytop and Phoenix House all refer to communities of this kind, and there are also numerous more recent projects of this type in the American prison system. They are also known as Concept Houses. Communities of this type are almost exclusively concerned with the rehabilitation of drug addicts, although attempts have been made to treat other offenders in this way.

Alternative Asylum and Anti-Psychiatry Communities

Dissatisfaction with conventional psychiatry and a concern with the spiritual, moral and social aspects of emotional distress have given rise to a number of communities which offer an alternative to mental hospital treatment. Some of these have been described as therapeutic communities. They do not form a single type, but tend to share certain features in common. These include a strong commitment to a particular faith or philosophy of life, and an emphasis on the equal status of all members. There are usually no labels of 'staff' or 'patient'. It is also characteristic of those communities which arose from the anti-psychiatry movement that a member can experience a psychotic breakdown without having it treated as an illness.

COMMON ATTRIBUTES

Allowing for exceptions, it seems generally true that those who have used the term therapeutic community have done so with similar principles and procedures in mind. I will start with the attributes that are most immediately obvious to the observer.

An Informal and Communal Atmosphere

This is often the first thing to strike a visitor or newcomer to a therapeutic community. The atmosphere is homelike rather than institutional, casual, perhaps untidy. People are dressed informally, no suits, no uniforms. The visitor wonders, 'Who are the staff?' What is absent is the atmosphere of listless boredom common in institutions, or the brisk white-coated efficiency of a general hospital. Neither is it a hushed clinic. Things are going on all around, not behind closed doors. Although informal, the atmosphere may not be relaxed – argument, laughter, tears are all possible. All out in the open where anyone can see or even join in. The newcomer is uneasily aware that some basic and expected boundaries have ceased to operate. Residents and staff are not clearly and immediately distinguishable. Events of a rather private nature seem to be going on in public. The lack of boundaries may be more apparent than real. On further acquaintance the visitor may learn that the staff do exert authority, or that the rather public airing of private feelings involves a certain amount of display by a particular individual. Yet the atmosphere of informality is real enough, and has much in common with the principle of 'Communalism' described by Rapoport in his book *Community as Doctor* (1960). He named this as one of four general principles to which therapeutic communities adhere.

The Central Place of Group Meetings in the Therapeutic Programme

These may take various forms but there will be regular times, at least once a week, often daily, when the whole community meets, and other times when members meet in smaller groups. The purpose and sophistication of these meetings will vary considerably from one community to another, and the goals may not always be fully stated or even recognized. Regardless of the type of community, however, the occurrence of these regular meetings, especially of the whole community, helps to fulfil the following functions:

(1)   *Maximize the sharing of information* Simply by being there, everyone is kept up to date, while anyone who has information to impart to the rest of the community (whether reporting events or giving opinions) has an effective means of doing so. The community meeting is in this sense a kind of living newspaper of the community.

(2) *Build a sense of cohesion and togetherness within the community* Everyone can see and get to know something about everyone else, can share in the hopes and fears expressed by other members, and in the day-to-day problems and achievements of the community.

(3) *Make open and public the process of decision making* In some communities, residents and staff decide jointly what to do about a particular matter affecting one of them or the community as a whole. In others, certain decisions may be made by the leader of the community, or by the staff together, but in both situations the way decisions are taken is visible to the whole community. This contrasts with the 'Kafkaesque' quality of many institutions where decisions emanate from secret places and are then handed down in such a manner that the recipient feels helpless to do anything about it should he disagree: a situation familiar both to staff and inmates of many traditional institutions.

(4) *Provide a forum for personal 'feedback'* Group meetings provide a situation where people can give and get personal reactions from one another, where participants can learn how they are seen not just by one other person but by many, and where as a result they can try to be less aggressive/demanding/self-effacing, to listen more/take more interest in others/or whatever change is suggested by the others

(5) Allied to this, group meetings provide *a vehicle for community members to exert pressure on individuals* whose attitudes or behaviour are disturbing or upsetting to others, or threaten their own well-being. This is going one step further than simply giving feedback, which the individual can choose to accept or ignore. In one community the pressure might be in the form of an exhortation, 'Why don't you try asking more politely next time you want to change the TV channel?' In another it might take the form of being put on 'probation' in the community, or being given a 'contract' to change a particular way of behaving.

Beyond these five common functions of group meetings, different types of therapeutic communities may employ other methods of group therapy selected from the wide range of techniques presently available, including group analytic therapy, cognitive behavioural techniques, psychodrama and art therapy.

Sharing the Work of Maintaining and Running the Community

This may vary from, at one extreme, residents doing virtually everything – cooking, cleaning, decorating, laundry, shopping, administration – to the other where hospital patients may help in serving meals and washing-up but leave most of the chores to paid staff. All therapeutic communities include some degree of real work; that is, work which contributes to the daily life of the community rather than work which is created in order to occupy the patients. Such work is important for several reasons:

(1)   Participating in the community's daily tasks helps members to feel part of the community, to feel it is their community. By contributing to its upkeep they are recognized as valued members of the community.

(2)   People who have never learned to lead independent, responsible lives can begin to acquire the necessary skills and confidence to use them.

(3)   Working with others in ordinary everyday tasks will bring to light many interpersonal problems which might remain dormant in group meetings. Reluctance to share or co-operate with someone else, fear of responsibility, insistence on always doing things one's own way, lack of persistence, may all emerge more clearly in a shared task of work than in a group discussion. Having emerged, these difficulties can then be examined in group meetings.

(4)   In addition to its immediate practical or therapeutic merits, participation in shared communal tasks also expresses the broader social values of social responsibility and citizenship, with the therapeutic community acting as a microcosm for the wider society.

The Therapeutic Role of Patients and Residents

The fourth common feature is the recognition of patients or residents as auxiliary therapists, commenting on and influencing each other's behaviour and attitudes. Naturally this goes on between the members of any community, even in the wards of a general hospital, but often in an 'unofficial' way: at mealtimes or during leisure activities. In a therapeutic community, deliberate use is made of the effectiveness of this informal source of influence.

Members of a therapeutic community are encouraged to take responsibility for thinking and deciding about matters which affect not only themselves but their residents too. New candidates for admission may be assessed by a mixed group of staff and residents. Once admitted, residents assess their own and each other's progress. Is Joan ready to go and look for a job? Should Roger visit his parents this weekend? Is Mary really depressed or is she just trying to get all the attention? When such questions are discussed, for example in a community meeting, many processes are going on. The person in focus is being confronted with interpretations of their behaviour as it is seen by their own peers, the other residents. Since some of them may be in the same situation, they can understand the problems and also see through excuses and false impressions. Rapoport (1960) called this the principle of Reality Confrontation. At the same time the experience of taking a therapeutic role towards others can help to develop self-confidence and self-esteem, which are often lacking in people with psychiatric or emotional problems. A further bonus is that residents may be better at explaining things to fellow residents because they use ordinary language rather than the jargon that professionals often use.

Sharing Authority

Linked to the role of auxiliary therapist is the more general sharing of authority by staff and residents. Residents are involved to a greater or lesser degree in the various decisions which have to be made in the running of the community. These may include the planning of community activities such as cooking a meal, going on an outing, organizing sports and social events. They may involve the relations between the community and outsiders – how many visitors the community can accommodate in one day, how to improve relationships with the neighbours. They may concern matters of income and expenditure – raising money for a new record player, finding the cheapest place to buy food, deciding how to spend a welcome donation.

Such decisions can be shared in different ways. In communities which subscribe to an egalitarian form of power sharing, decisions may be made on the principle of one person one vote, regardless of status, or on the basis of a consensus with attention being paid to the views of all. In the latter situation some members may be more influential than others, but the principle is that everyone should have the opportunity to take part in the decision-making process. The other form of sharing is a hierarchy in which certain decisions are delegated downwards. For instance, the director of a community delegates responsibility for different tasks to junior staff, who in turn delegate to residents the responsibility for such activities as preparing meals or cleaning the house. They in turn may delegate particular jobs to others.

It is important to recognize that although the first form may appear to be more democratic, both represent ways of giving residents real responsibility in relation to the day-to-day management of the community.

Values and Beliefs

So far the common attributes have been those concerned with 'practice' – with the daily events and routines of therapeutic communities. In addition to these there are certain 'values' or beliefs that characterize such communities. In saying what these are I am aware that different types of therapeutic communities may consider themselves to have different – even opposing – values. We might find this if we talked with members of 'democratic' and 'hierarchical' communities. Nevertheless it seems to me that it is possible to identify some basic ideals or points of view that are shared by all therapeutic communities.

First is 'the belief inherent in most psychotherapy and psychological treatment that *an individual's difficulties are mostly in relation with other people'* (Clark 1965). Symptoms such as anxiety or depression, or disorders of behaviour such as delinquency and self-destructive acts, are seen as the outward expression of emotional conflicts and tensions in an individual's relations with others. This view, that symptoms have meaning, that irrational behaviour can be understood, stems from the work of Freud and psychoanalysis. While not all therapeutic communities espouse psychoanalytic ideas, and some may draw on other therapeutic models (e.g. transactional analysis, cognitive behaviour therapy), most would agree that one special advantage of therapeutic communities is the opportunity they provide for observing the connection between psychological disturbance in an individual and changes in his relationships with others.

A second shared belief is that *therapy is essentially a learning process*: both in the sense of knowledge – learning about oneself and others – and skills – learning how to relate to others, for example how to be more open or more assertive. This view of therapy is fundamentally different from the medical view in which the patient is a relatively passive recipient of treatment, and 'cure' or 'failure' is dependent upon the skill of the doctor and nurses. In a therapeutic community, as in other forms of psychotherapy, the process is more like that of education. The resident is in the position of a learner, who benefits most when he is interacting with the material to be learned. In this case the material includes the other people in the community and the individual's own thoughts and feelings.

A third shared value which characterises therapeutic communities is the *recognition of the basic equality of all members*, whether staff or residents, professionals or non-professionals, therapists or patients. This equality has two aspects, which may be called the human and the psychological. By *human equality* I am referring to the belief that we should treat others as we would like to be treated, that we should not exploit others or unduly restrict their rights or freedom. Where such freedoms are restricted – e.g. insistence on attending group meetings, not allowing community members to enter into a sexual relationship – this should be through the consensus of the community as being in the interests of the individuals affected or of the community as a whole.

Psychological equality is the recognition that all members, whatever their role, share many of the same psychological processes. To put this in the context of a hospital, staff are not completely 'well' and patients are not completely 'sick'. Staff members can at times feel upset, anxious, or helpless; patients can at times be caring, creative, and competent. Neither side has a monopoly of strengths or weaknesses. This contrasts with the view found in more traditional care settings, where the providers and recipients of care usually find it comfortable to adopt the complementary roles of helper and helpless, ignoring those parts of themselves that do not fit with these roles – a custom so widespread in our society that it can occur in therapeutic communities too, especially among new members.

The belief in basic equality should not be taken as saying that there are no differences between the helpers and the helped, but rather that in a therapeutic community the other bits of oneself can also be shown. Staff members can admit to feelings which fall outside the conventional staff role – e.g. frustration or confusion – and patients can 'admit' to areas of skill and understanding that do not qualify as usual patient attributes. Striking a good balance between acknowledging the equality of staff and residents and maintaining the necessary differences in their roles is a crucial and sometimes difficult aspect of staff training.

The final common value is difficult to define. One thing of which newcomers are sometimes aware is the sense of entering a 'closed order' to which they do not belong and where certain things are not open to question. For example, all the talk about openness and honesty may not seem to include permission to question the value of having a therapeutic community – which is just what the newcomer often wants to do. While much of this feeling may be what a newcomer experiences in any situation, there is also a sense in which therapeutic communities do represent a moral statement for those who work in them. By this I mean that the various principles and procedures described in this chapter have developed not only because they have been found to be therapeutically effective, but because they also express certain beliefs about relationships, about how people ought to treat each other and how professional workers ought (and ought not) to treat their clients.

Tom Main eloquently expressed such beliefs in the article which first introduced the term therapeutic community:

> The anarchical rights of the doctor in the traditional hospital society have to be exchanged for the more sincere role of member in a real community, responsible not only to himself and his superiors, but to the community as a whole, privileged and restricted only insofar as the community allows or demands. He no longer owns 'his' patients. They are given up to the community which is to treat them, and which owns them and him. Patients are no longer his captive children, obedient in nursery-like activities, but have sincere adult roles to play, and are free to reach for responsibilities and opinions concerning the community of which they are a part. (Main 1946)

Although most therapeutic communities are non-religious, the presence of this moral component can be traced back a long way, to the Quaker convictions of the early pioneers who laid the foundations from which modern therapeutic communities derive. In the next chapter we trace the development of moral treatment, which was the first attempt to create a special social environment for the humane treatment of people suffering from severe disorders of the mind.

The existence of a strong moral or ideological aspect to therapeutic communities can be seen as both an asset and a risk. It is an asset because it contributes to a high level of enthusiasm and commitment among the staff and residents. The instillation of hope and raising of morale are an important part of any therapeutic enterprise (Frank 1979) and the moral value which therapeutic community members attach to their approach gives it a headstart in this respect. The risk is that this commitment may slip over into idealization of the community and a refusal to listen to criticism or acknowledge limitations. There is a risk of therapeutic communities becoming 'Messianic', seeing themselves as guardians of the 'truth' (Hobson 1979). Learning to strike the right balance between moral conviction and openness to self-appraisal is a difficult task faced by all those who work in the helping professions. It is particularly so in a therapeutic community, where work and values are closely bound up with each other.

CHAPTER 2

The Rise and Fall
of Moral Treatment

The enthusiastic way in which the idea of a therapeutic community was first taken up in Britain in the 1950s, and later in other countries, had a lot to do with its being seen an antidote to traditional institutions for people with chronic mental illness. These institutions had changed little during the first half of the twentieth century, but following a string of critical investigations in Britain and the United States they had become infamous for their regimentation, the lack of initiative or individuality they allowed, and for their purely custodial nature (Stanton and Schwartz 1954, Bockoven 1956, Barton 1959, Goffman 1961). In attempting to change these institutions a handful of courageous hospital superintendents were inspired by the idea of a therapeutic community, where patients could take an active part in their own rehabilitation, learning social and work skills long forgotten, and where staff could facilitate, encourage and lead rather than restrict, punish and prevent.

More recently many of these pioneering hospital-based therapeutic communities have been overtaken by sweeping hospital closure programmes that portray all institutional care in a negative light. Perhaps it was inevitable that once it started, the bandwagon against institutional care would roll over everyone, including those who had tried, and succeeded, to make it better. The irony in this situation has been expressed by Roy Porter: 'Our age, which has seen the agitation for the closing of traditional asylums come to fruition, has also been the time when many of them have been, at long last, most therapeutically innovative and successful' (Porter 1996). The need for caring asylum, whether in a large institution or in more ordinary locally based housing, has not gone away, and we must take care not to lose what was learnt in the years when institutions became a force for therapeutic innovation.

Such changes were not easily brought about, and the efforts, even when successful, were not always lasting. A therapeutic community is not a static piece of equipment but a way of relating and communicating – never easy, never automatic, always in danger of succumbing to administrative convenience.

In order to appreciate the origins of the therapeutic community in an institution, we need to take a detour into the more distant history of psychiatry, for this was not the first time that its practitioners had tried to overcome wretched conditions and neglectful care.

The background story to the idea of running an institution for the mentally ill as a therapeutic community goes back to the turn of the eighteenth and nineteenth centuries. It was a time of widespread social upheaval. The American war of Independence and the French Revolution were recent events, and in England social reformers were active in championing the rights of the underprivileged and oppressed. In this context there was a great interest in the welfare and treatment of the 'insane', who until that time had been lumped together with other groups of social deviants unable to care for themselves or regarded as a nuisance to society – vagrants, petty criminals, the physically handicapped and the destitute poor. Such people were usually kept at home with their families, or else in one of the custodial institutions of the time – the poorhouse, the workhouse, the madhouse, the 'hospital' (a medieval concept, that was ecclesiastical not medical) or the gaol.

Concern for the fate of mentally disturbed people, especially those confined to squalid madhouses where inmates were sometimes kept chained to the wall, led to the development of a new method of treatment known as 'moral treatment'. Despite its rather – to our ears – quaint name, moral treatment included many of the elements which today form part of the essential basis of any therapeutic community – especially those for the rehabilitation of long-term psychiatric patients.

What is remarkable is that having made its appearance and flourished for a few decades – until around the middle of the nineteenth century – moral treatment then faded. It disappeared into the brickwork, so to speak, of the very institutions which had been built largely in its name. When therapeutic communities began making their appearance in large mental hospitals in the years following World War II, they were in some respects reviving a way of running those institutions that had laid dormant for nearly a hundred years. Three questions are of interest to us here. How did moral treatment come about? What was it? Why did it disappear?

HOW DID MORAL TREATMENT COME ABOUT?[1]

When a Quaker patient, Hannah Mills, died mysteriously in the York Asylum in 1790 the incident so disturbed the local Quaker community that they decided to create their own establishment for Friends – fellow Quakers – suffering 'the loss of reason'. Championed by William Tuke, a Quaker tea and coffee merchant, the York Retreat opened in 1796. It took thirty patients. Over the next twenty years Tuke developed an approach that had a profound effect on the treatment of the insane as practised at that time. In place of physical restraints and enforced idleness, common in eighteenth-century madhouses, he showed how treating the insane as near as possible as normal people and giving them useful occupations could produce unimagined improvement in their mental state.

The term moral treatment was originally used by the revolutionary French physician Pinel to refer to 'treatment through the emotions', and was borrowed by Samuel Tuke (William's grandson) when trying to explain the methods of The Retreat in a book he published in 1813, simply called *Description of The Retreat*. Tuke's use of the term was not a hundred miles from what we would recognize today as the aim of most forms of psychological intervention. To quote Tuke, moral treatment focused on the means by which 'the power of the patient to control the disorder is strengthened and assisted'. In dealing with serious mental disorder, moral treatment also dealt with what 'modes of coercion' should be used 'when restraint is absolutely necessary' (Tuke 1813, p.138). In contrast to the previous practice of the times, in which any form of restraint had been considered acceptable because the insane were not thought to be fully human, Tuke, with his Quaker concept of personhood, argued for minimum restraint and for the acceptance of risk in the management of disturbed behaviour. He was well aware of the ethical issues involved. The use of social reinforcement was also clearly recognized: Tuke pointed out that providing a comfortable environment increased the patient's 'desire to restrain himself by exciting the wish not to forfeit his enjoyments' (Tuke 1813, p.177).

Moral treatment as first developed at The Retreat was aimed at recognizing and nurturing the intact part of the patient's personality, through whatever methods were available. At the time these methods were the use of social expectation, kind and humane relationships, and some elements of social reward, although a number of our present day approaches – in particular humanistic, cognitive and behavioural – would be quite compatible with the basic aim.

---

1   I would like to thank Annie Borthwick, resident Friend at The Retreat, for her helpful comments on the following sections.

The success of The Retreat was well publicized and helped to set in motion intense debates about existing institutions for the mentally ill. Parliamentary inquiries led to a series of laws which, by 1845, required every county in England to provide for its 'pauper lunatics' a purpose-built asylum. Advocates of this approach firmly believed that it was best conducted away from the site of the original difficulties – the insane person's home – in the calming sanctuary of a well-run asylum. Meanwhile visitors came from many countries and some returned home determined to use Tuke's ideas.

In 1817 a hospital modelled on the York Retreat was founded in the United States by the Pennsylvania Quakers. However, the situation in America was very different from the one in England. They did not have the widespread tradition of private and charity institutions for social deviants that existed in England, the abuses in which had led directly to the founding of the York Retreat. The concerns of the new Americans, following the 1776 Declaration of Independence, were to do with the creation of a new type of society – the first democratic republic. They wanted to demonstrate to themselves and the rest of the world that such social problems as crime and insanity could be overcome in their new type of society. Paradoxically, many Americans believed that life in this new society of unlimited opportunities led to increased likelihood of mental breakdown. Doctors warned that when people overreached their capacities the result was insanity. For these doctors moral treatment meant placing the victim of these social pressures in an environment designed to restore inner equilibrium. In their asylums they attempted to create a new, ideal mini-society in which the virtues of order, calm and productive work would replace the chaos and competitiveness of a burgeoning new world. (See Rothman (1971) for a full account of the development of moral treatment in the United States.)

Thus for quite different reasons moral treatment caught on in America and England in the early nineteenth century – in England to counter the abuses of a long-established pattern of containment in private madhouses and charity asylums; in America to counter the distressing effects of contemporary society on its more vulnerable members. Although attempts to create Utopian communities were also taking place in England at this time, these had little to do with contemporary efforts to reform the treatment of the insane. Indeed English reformers were themselves sceptical of the view that social conditions could cause insanity. Yet despite their different beliefs about the causes of insanity, and despite their different motives for wanting to bring about a radical change in the treatment of the insane, the English and American reformers developed a remarkably similar approach. In both countries the enthusiasm of the proponents of moral treatment led to an increasing number of asylums being built for the express purpose of conducting this form of treatment, and for a time it seemed as though the solution to insanity had been found.

WHAT WAS MORAL TREATMENT?

Moral treatment can be described in three ways: as an ideology, as a practice, and as a set of principles about the treatment of mental illness.

Ideology

By ideology I mean the views about the way society ought to be organized, and about the consequences of organizing it one way or another – in this case with particular reference to the treatment of mental disorder. Two different ideologies supported the development of moral treatment, one in America and one in England. American psychiatrists in the nineteenth century, medical superintendents of the new asylums for the mentally ill, believed that contemporary society was often psychologically harmful, and that the answer lay not in changing that society, but in creating asylums in which a new social order would rehabilitate the casualties of the system, by being designed 'in the reverse image of the world they had left'. The idea that a community created in the 'reverse image' of society at large can be therapeutic for the casualties of that society, is an appealing one that links moral treatment with the history of therapeutic communities. In both, the same logic can be employed: if one kind of social environment produces mental distress, the opposite kind of social environment will heal it. Some therapeutic communities for children and adolescents have particularly followed this logic (see Chapter 3 for further details).

A quite different ideology was espoused by Tuke. Unlike America, where moral treatment was pioneered by medical doctors, in England it developed as a challenge to the medical profession, or at least to those doctors who profited by claiming to be experts in the treatment of the insane. Andrew Scull, in his book 'Museums of Madness', writes that

> Tuke had explicitly not sought to create or train a group of experts in moral treatment. He and his followers were deeply suspicious of any plan to hand the treatment of lunatics over to experts. In the words of William Ellis (the superintendent of one of the new moral treatment asylums), 'Of the abuses that have existed, the cause of a great proportion of them may be traced to the mystery with which many of those who have had the management of the insane have constantly endeavoured to envelop it'. Those who had developed moral treatment claimed that the new approach was little more than an application of common sense and humanity; and these were scarcely qualities monopolized by experts. (Scull 1979, p.142)

In other words, the advocates of moral treatment in England had an ideology which dispensed with 'expertise' on two counts: it had been used to conceal harmful practices, and it was unnecessary because what the insane needed could be given by anyone with the right attitude and personal qualities.

The emergence of the therapeutic community movement was accompanied by similar arguments. In 1946 Tom Main wrote that the doctor had to give up his 'anarchical rights' in exchange for 'the more sincere role of member in a real community'. This ideology had a negative consequence for moral treatment, as it has for therapeutic communities. Both have suffered from lack of professional recognition, being marginalized by the more established professions. The controversy still goes on, and we discuss the pros and cons of training in Chapter 13.

Practice

The basic practice of moral treatment sounds simple enough to our ears: engage the disturbed individual in a regular routine of useful, varied work, and do this within an intimate, family-like atmosphere in an attractive setting and location. Yet this at the time was revolutionary. Prior to moral treatment, institutions for the insane had been noted for the enforced idleness of inmates who were often chained or manacled, and lived in filthy overcrowded cells, where the smell could make a visitor vomit. The pioneers of moral treatment in England intended to show that physical restraint was rarely needed and that insanity was curable, not by any of the then current medical treatments such as bleeding or purging, but by ordinary employment in everyday tasks, which restored order and tranquillity to the mind. These included farming, gardening, household tasks and simple workshop tasks. The particular task mattered less than the way it was carried out. A precise and regular routine would bring order to disordered lives. Regular employment would encourage patients in self-restraint, take their minds off their problems, and encourage the regular work habits which would turn them into productive members of society.

Equally important was the atmosphere in which these activities were carried out. Patients were treated as if they were normal, rational beings. Staff tolerated disturbed behaviour as much as possible, and used solitude or physical restraint only as a last resort. The overall atmosphere was meant to resemble an extended family, with the asylum superintendent as its head. The role of the superintendent was of central importance:

> By paying minute attention to all aspects of the day-to-day conduct of the institution, by always setting through his example a high standard for subordinates to emulate in their dealing with the inmates, he could foster the kind of intimate and benevolent familiar environment in which acts of violence would naturally become rare. (Scull 1979)

Principles
The curability of insanity

Prior to the era of moral treatment it was generally assumed that madness was incurable. Beliefs about its cause varied: the will of God, possession by evil spirits, an imbalance of the 'humours', a hereditary disease passed on through the blood. The attitude to treatment was in all cases the same. Once struck, the unfortunate victim could only be cared for or, if dangerous, sent away or locked up. Occasional physical remedies were applied by doctors, of the kind applied to patients with fever, but the results were not encouraging. The single greatest change brought about by moral treatment was the new belief, and the demonstration, that insanity was curable, and that its cure lay not in the erudite realm of medicine but in the everyday realm of the patient's daily routine and social environment. The founders of The Retreat believed, like all Quakers, that there was 'that of God' in every individual. In approaching someone who had lost their reason the same belief held that, regardless of the degree of disturbance, there was an 'inner light' – an essential spiritual core – which, if it could be reached, could bring the person back into normal relations with himself and others.

The biggest achievement of moral treatment was not that it provided a successful treatment for mental illness but that it changed the task of the asylum from custody to rehabilitation. It was a change which would have to be repeated in later years.

Reward rather than punish

The moral treatment pioneers acted on the assumption that patients were amenable to social inducements to behave acceptably, to the praise, encouragement and the esteem of others. Severe discipline and harsh restraints were not only inhumane, they were seen as unnecessary. Patients would respond according to the staff's expectations: treat them as uncontrollable madmen and that is how they will behave, treat them as rational, responsible beings and they will act accordingly. One measure of this change in approach was the amazement of visitors to the new asylums on seeing patients allowed to handle knives and sharp farm implements.

The success of moral treatment as a new and better way of treating the mentally ill – not only more humane but more effective – was repeatedly emphasized by its advocates. Yet critics of moral treatment, like Scull, have pointed out that it could also be regarded as a method of moulding patients into the kind of citizens that suited society.

> The insane were to be restored to reason by a system of rewards and punishment not essentially different from those used to teach a young child to obey the dictates of 'civilized' morality ... the lunatics were to be

made over in the image of bourgeois rationality: defective human mechanisms were to be repaired so that they could once more compete in the marketplace. (Scull 1979)

It can be argued that Scull wrongly equated Quaker and bourgois values, and that the kind of conformity Quakers were seeking was to values that were different from those of mainstream society. Today, Scull's criticisms can be and are made of therapeutic communities, and of other forms of psychiatric treatment too – that they are intended to bring about social conformity. Perhaps the strongest evidence for this – and the dilemma it created – was in the two world wars when humane psychiatrists struggled with their consciences as they treated soldiers suffering from 'shell-shock' or post traumatic stress.[2] However, what such critics often ignore is that it is difficult for an individual to live in society without conforming at least to certain basic norms and values.

The importance of size and setting

In order to create an intimate family-like atmosphere the number of inmates and staff in an asylum had to be kept small. The ideal was considered to be a total of between 100 and 120 – at most 200 – divided into units of about ten people. This would correspond to a large extended family, small enough for patients to have all the individual care they required, and all be personally known to the superintendent. Moral treatment could not be carried out, its advocates argued, when the numbers in an asylum grew too large for an intimate, family atmosphere to exist. These warnings were not heeded, as we shall see.

The reformers in England and America also believed that the physical construction and setting of the asylum were crucial to the success of treatment. So much so, in fact, that many medical superintendents became obsessed with the details of building and design. They required the asylum to be located far away from the disturbing influence of city life, in a soothing rustic setting with pleasant views and walks. Since they believed that the patient's social environment – usually a town or city – had contributed to his breakdown, it was logical to them that recovery required as big a separation from this environment as possible. For the same reason visits from friends and relatives were generally discouraged. It is interesting to realize that these are the reasons why nineteenth-century mental hospitals were located away

---

2   This has been dramatically portrayed in Pat Barker's novel set in the First World War, *Regeneration*, made into a film in 1997. In describing the Northfield therapeutic community experiment in World War II, Bion acknowledged that 'one of the difficulties facing a psychiatrist who is treating combatant soldiers is his feeling of guilt that he is trying to bring them to a state of mind in which they will have to face dangers, not excluding loss of life, that he himself is not called upon to face' (Bion 1946).

from centres of population; today we often assume that this was solely in order to rid city dwellers of the discomfort of having people who were mad in their midst.

The personal attributes of the staff

Moral treatment laid great emphasis on having enough staff to give individual care to patients. In the better establishments they numbered as many as one for every four or five patients. It was recognized that the attendant was the person who had the most extensive and intimate contact with the patient. Personal qualities were therefore of great importance, and the new superintendents paid a lot of attention to selecting the right kind of staff. They had to be kind, intelligent, of upright character and with an unusual degree of forbearance. There was apparently no shortage of suitable applicants. Young men and women of respectable families, adequate education and 'refined moral feelings' were often prepared to devote a few years to asylum employment. Compared with the years before, and immediately following moral treatment, it was an era of remarkable social responsiveness to the needs of the mentally ill.

WHY DID MORAL TREATMENT DISAPPEAR?

Many reasons have been put forward to explain why this humane and apparently successful approach should have all but vanished by the time the last county asylums were being built in the 1890s. No one explanation alone will do, and it would be hard to say which, if any, was the decisive one. In one sense, it was killed by its own success as a reform movement. Social reformers, pointing to the success of the early attempts at moral treatment, persuaded the English Parliament and the American States to provide similar institutions on an increasingly large scale. In doing so they ignored the vital matter of the size of the asylum. In order to cater for all the insane – not only those in madhouses but those presently looked after by their families – an upper limit of 200 was stretched to 300, then to 500, then 1000 and finally vast mental hospitals containing 2–3000 patients were constructed. With such numbers the aim of establishing a family atmosphere was left far behind.

The type of patient began to change too. In the middle decades of the nineteenth century there was a huge increase in the number of immigrants arriving in America from Europe, and one effect of this was to swell the numbers admitted to the asylums. The goal of creating a stable, well-ordered society became increasingly remote, both within and outside the asylum. In England a law passed in 1890 required that only the most incurable should be admitted to hospital. Such changes tended to push asylums towards a more custodial role on both sides of the Atlantic.

Another reason for the decline of moral treatment was Tuke and his followers' aversion (referred to earlier) to establishing a new profession of 'experts' in moral treatment. This meant that there was no coherent challenge to the claims of the medical profession to be the natural authority responsible for the mentally ill. In this context Kathleen Jones (1996) noted the fate of Samuel Tuke's *Description of The Retreat*. For the twenty-five years following its publication in 1813 it was the standard British textbook on the subject of patient care and treatment. However, 'the asylum doctors were very conscious of their medical status, and they looked for medical antecedents'. They found them in Pinel, the contemporary Parisian doctor whose term *'traitement moral'* Tuke had borrowed but whose approach was actually quite different. The medical profession soon adopted Pinel as the originator of moral therapy, and no reference to Tuke or The Retreat appeared in key medical books and journals published after 1837.

As the original pioneers retired, died or became disillusioned, their efforts died with them. Disillusion must have been produced not only by the increasing size of the institutions but also by the discovery in the latter half of the nineteenth century that many of the earlier claims to success had been exaggerated. This had the effect of discrediting the success that had been achieved. Meanwhile, different views of the nature of mental illness were beginning to prevail. Interest was shifting towards a search for organic causes, giving psychiatry renewed hope of achieving its goal of recognition as a proper medical discipline. Although this search was relatively unsuccessful, it meant that moral treatment, with its emphasis on social and humanitarian factors, had become an outmoded and apparently discredited approach by the end of the nineteenth century.

One aspect of moral treatment which survived only too well in the new enlarged asylums was the emphasis on supervision and inspection. Originally this had been introduced to ensure that the abuses of the madhouse were not repeated and that attendants were treating patients with proper tolerance and encouragement. But supervision in a personal, family-like setting is very different from supervision in a large institution. Shorn of its original role as one part of moral treatment, inspection grew to be an all-pervading obsession in many large asylums.

By the beginning of the twentieth century all that was left of the era of moral treatment was a collection of asylums whose size alone condemned them to a life of routine and regimentation. With the passing of moral treatment so too passed the belief in the treatability of mental illness. The country air and the views, once thought beneficial for the mentally disturbed town dweller, now ensured that his plight was forgotten by all except those who had direct contact with the institution. The world of the asylum changed little in the first half of the twentieth century. Attempts were made in the 1930s by some Dutch and English psychiatrists to introduce work programmes to counteract the effects of institutional boredom and lethargy. But in the 1950s a Boston psychiatrist named J.S. Bockoven described a ward in an American mental hospital as follows:

> It is not until one enters the wards where the patients live that one feels the impact of what it means to be a patient in a typical mental hospital. Contrary to one's expectations, ward after ward may be passed through without witnessing the violent, the grotesque, or the ridiculous. Instead, one absorbs the heavy atmosphere of hundreds of people doing nothing and showing interest in nothing. Endless lines of people sit on benches along the walls. Some have their eyes closed; others gaze fixedly at the floor or the opposite wall. Occasionally a head is turned to look out of a window or to watch someone coming back from the toilet to take his place on a bench. All in all, it is an innocuous scene characterised by inertness, listlessness, docility, and utter hopelessness. (Bockoven 1956)

The attitude of the staff reveals a faint and distorted echo from the days of moral treatment:

> The visitor learns that the attendant is proud of the ward because it is quiet and no mishaps have occurred while he was on duty; because the floor is clean; because the patients are prompt and orderly in going to and from meals. The visitor finds that the scene which appalls him with the emptiness and pointlessness of human life is regarded by the attendant as good behaviour on the part of the patients. (Bockoven 1956)

THE EMERGENCE OF THE INSTITUTIONAL THERAPEUTIC COMMUNITY

The attempt to introduce therapeutic community principles into large mental hospitals was the result of a number of forces which converged together in Britain in the 1950s. Prior to this there was a handful of hospital superintendents who, aware of the earlier success of moral treatment, had tried to reduce the hospital's custodial role, although not attempting a complete reorganization. At Dingleton Hospital the doors to the wards were unlocked; at Mapperly the nurses began to work with patients outside the hospital; at Warlingham Park the influential hospital superintendent T.P. Rees encouraged junior psychiatrists to conduct group meetings on the wards. Two of these, Bertram Mandelbrote and Denis Martin, went on to play leading roles in the application of therapeutic community principles in large institutions (Martin 1962, Mandelbrote 1965, Freeman 1965).

But the adoption of a therapeutic community approach to running an institution was more than a re-emergence of moral treatment. Four other factors played an important part. One was the inspiration provided by the new, small, specialized therapeutic communities that had developed during and since World War II, which are discussed in detail in the next chapter. Maxwell Jones, who developed the best known of these new units at Belmont Hospital in Surrey, was an active support and mentor to David Clark when in 1953 he became the youngest psychiatrist to be appointed as a medical superintendent at the large and rundown Fulbourne Hospital at Cambridge (Clark 1996). At the time, most psychiatrists believed that therapeutic communities were only suitable for psychopaths but Jones believed the model had broader applicability. He encouraged Clark and his colleague to try developing them for patients suffering from chronic psychoses, and in 1962 Jones took the job of superintendent at Dingleton Hospital on the Scottish borders to try this for himself (Jones 1982, Clark 1997).

A second influence was the emergence of a trend related to therapeutic communities – group therapy. Two psychoanalysts who had become interested in leading groups in the course of wartime therapeutic community experiments continued to exert a significant influence on mental health workers in the post-war years. They were W.R. Bion, who led study groups at the Tavistock Clinic, and S.H. Foulkes, the originator of group analysis, who worked at the Maudsley Hospital, London's leading psychiatric teaching hospital. Psychiatrists like Clark and Mandelbrote while training at the Maudsley had the opportunity to gain first-hand group experience which they were later able to use in getting patients and staff to meet and discuss their mutual concerns.

A third important force in this period of rethinking about asylums was the sociological research in American psychiatric hospitals by Stanton and Schwartz (1954), Caudill (1958), and above all Goffman (1961). They studied the social behaviour of patients in mental hospitals. They observed how an unexpressed conflict between members of staff on a ward could lead to disturbed behaviour amongst the patients; how failure to deal openly with a source of collective tension result in mutual withdrawal of patients and staff and then an outbreak of collective disturbance; how the relationships among patients and between staff and patients could be understood in terms of the social effects of living in what Goffman called a 'total institution' – where every aspect of life takes place within the asylum. Not only were these studies fascinating, they also provided a rationale for trying to change the way the institutions were run. Above all they showed the importance of open communications in order to avoid the build-up of tension around hidden issues of conflict. They also indicated that behaviour could be understood in terms of how patients and staff adjusted to the social 'system' of the hospital, not just in terms of individual illness or personality. To change people, then, it might be necessary to understand and change the social organization of the ward or hospital.

Such ideas gave impetus to the therapeutic community approach. In England, impetus also came from a fourth factor, the creation in 1948 of the National Health Service. There was a challenge to do something about the thousands of seemingly untreatable people with chronic schizophrenia who filled the mental hospitals, and there were the resources and enthusiasm to make things work.

It may not be a coincidence that the therapeutic community approach to asylum populations has often been tried in the wake of wider social changes. Moral treatment itself arose in the wake of the American and French revolutions. Cuba and Israel provide two examples of new societies created in the second half of the twentieth century where a therapeutic community approach emerged naturally as part of a new approach to traditional problems. More recently, Italy has proved another example of the emergence of a therapeutic community approach in the wake of a radical change in its mental health services, in this case the passing in 1978 of the famous Law 180 which at a stroke banned further admissions to psychiatric hospitals (Pedriali 1997). This may fall short of total revolution but it provided the essential ingredient – the belief that a new approach can overcome problems that the old 'regime' had found insoluble.

CHAPTER 3

Democracy, Psychoanalysis and Planned Environment Therapy

Moral treatment emphasized the need for a humane, caring, intimate environment in which disturbed or troublesome individuals could be treated with normal dignity and encouraged to lead orderly, productive lives. Beyond this humane paternalism two ideas have gripped the imagination of many pioneers working with the disturbed, the difficult and the deviant: participative democracy and psychoanalysis. In the quite different settings of schools for maladjusted children, psychiatric hospitals for adults who are emotionally disabled, and prisons for youthful, aggressive offenders, these pioneers have created regimes which bear a striking resemblance to one another.

Most widely shared has been the idea of giving the residents or inmates responsibility for deciding how they want the establishment to be run and then working out with them how this is to be done. This sharing of responsibility can achieve several goals. It undermines the expectation of being told what to do. Such an expectation tends to lead either to compliance or to rebellion, neither of which is helpful when the aim is for people to become more mature, responsible individuals. It also allows people to learn in a practical way the consequences of their decisions; and it brings them into a situation where in order to get things done they have to begin to co-operate with others, to see other people's points of view and to know how to put their own across in a reasonable way.

Such an approach provides enormous opportunities for increasing self-awareness and social maturity, yet it probably could not have come about before nineteenth-century morality had begun to yield to more liberal ideas. Four factors were important in counteracting the repressive Victorian response to social maladjustment and deviance. Two were not new: the Christian ideal of love of the person, no matter how bad the deed; and the democratic ideal of a republic in which all men are equal. These two ideals were provided with an invaluable ally in psychoanalysis, which emerged around the turn of the twentieth century and showed how irrational behaviour could be understood and, through understanding, changed. A fourth factor was the impetus that World War II gave to innovations in social psychiatry and social psychology which would not have arisen in less urgent times.

The term therapeutic community was first used to describe experiments which took place at a military psychiatric hospital during the early 1940s. However, many of the ingredients of these experiments had already been tried out with maladjusted children under the heading of 'Planned Environment Therapy'. Although not identical there are sufficient similarities between Planned Environment Therapy and therapeutic communities to warrant our devoting some attention to the former. Since both have been influenced by psychoanalysis, it may be helpful for those new to it to spend a page or two getting acquainted with this subject.

THE CONTRIBUTION OF PSYCHOANALYSIS

Psychoanalysis was created by Freud in the last decade of the nineteenth century as both a method for treating neuroses and a way of studying unconscious thoughts, feelings and experience. Both involved the method of free association, in which the patient was encouraged to say whatever came into his or her mind. In therapeutic communities this has its equivalent in the principle of permissiveness – allowing patients a wide range of freedom in their actions. Psychoanalysis also produced, and continues to elaborate in its various 'schools', a number of theories about the way personality develops. This promoted an important change in attitude towards social deviance and maladjustment, replacing authoritarian and punitive attitudes with ones which stressed empathy and understanding. Others too had stressed the need for love and understanding, but psychoanalysis provided a more complete theory about what it was that needed understanding. Those therapeutic community pioneers who were intuitively or ideologically inclined towards an equal sharing of roles and the mutual discussion of problems in living, found in the theories of Freud and his contemporaries a powerful rationale to support and guide their efforts. They also found a number of specific ideas which could either be applied 'straight' or adapted to the particular needs of a therapeutic community.

Broadly, therapeutic communities have made use of psychoanalytic ideas in three ways. One has been the practice of individual psychotherapy within a therapeutic community. The second has been the use of psychoanalytic concepts as a way of understanding and using individual relationships throughout the community. The third has been a psychoanalytic approach to understanding processes affecting the community as a whole – for example relationships between different sections of the community or between the community and the world outside it. Let us briefly consider each of these applications, and some of the concepts involved.

(1)   Psychoanalysis as a therapeutic method refers to a well-defined arrangement in which the psychoanalyst and patient meet together at a regular time four or five times a week, usually over a period of some years. The psychoanalyst participates in a relationship with the patient in which the patient is encouraged to say whatever comes into his or her mind. A modified version of this method has been used in some therapeutic communities for maladjusted children for whom a close relationship with an adult is needed before they can begin to relate to other children. It is rare in adult therapeutic communities, where it is the community with all its potential relationships which provides the therapy. However, there are notable examples of a combined approach – individual therapy and therapeutic community living – such as the Cassel Hospital. On the other hand, in-patient psychotherapy units, without a therapeutic community aspect, are found in a number of countries.

(2)   Relationships between the members of a therapeutic community are subject to a number of distorting influences which interfere with members' capacity to work together and enjoy one another's company. Many of these distortions can be attributed to involuntary psychological habits of thinking and feeling which members carry around with them, causing them to react inappropriately to people they meet. When these habits emerge in relationships within the community there is an opportunity to examine, understand and change them. Several psychoanalytic concepts are used in this process of understanding. 'Transference' refers to a relationship in which one person attributes to another qualities which belong in the person's relationships with important others, usually family members. 'Counter-transference' refers to the emotions experienced towards that person by those to whom the transference is directed. For example, someone who often felt disapproved of as a child may react to another member of the community as though they too were disapproving. Their way of dealing with this might be to try to win approval, provoking a reaction of irritation in other community members. Such a 'counter-transference' may confirm the original transference, setting up a chain or spiral of reactions. Here is a real life example:

A widow in her late fifties was admitted to hospital in a depressed, withdrawn state. There had been difficulties between her and her son and daughter, and they did not come to visit her in hospital. She started to complain that the staff were treating her badly. She refused to attend community meetings and on several occasions left the unit with the intention of walking home, a journey of several miles, in bad weather. Those staff who were most involved in containing her began to feel increasingly frustrated and exasperated, and found themselves becoming angry and unsympathetic towards her. This reaction confirmed her belief that she was being treated badly by the staff. When her children were persuaded to start visiting her she became much brighter and co-operative, and the staff felt relieved and warmer towards her.

The concepts of transference and counter-transference are valuable aids in understanding what otherwise might appear only as a difficult and inescapable 'vicious circle' between two or more people. Another source of interference in personal relationships occurs when one person attributes to another his own feelings or attitudes. This is called 'projection'. This usually occurs when a person has a feeling which, in his own eyes at least, is unacceptable. For example, if someone feels annoyed with you, instead of recognizing this he may instead perceive you as being annoyed with him.

Sometimes it happens that several people in a group or community project some unacceptable quality into one individual who is then attacked and driven out. This is known as 'scapegoating'. Often the individual concerned does possess the unacceptable quality to some degree, which on the surface can make the scapegoating seem reasonable. For example, an individual with a propensity for violent outbursts may be treated by everyone else as if he were the only person with a problem in controlling his anger, enabling others to ignore their own violent impulses. At times such occurrences may have their constructive side, as when a member of the community is confronted by the others over his antisocial behaviour. Being alert to the possibility of projection and scapegoating can help to reduce their harmful effects, and may enable people to become more aware of their own feelings.

The staff team of one therapeutic community was characterized by a casual, almost cavalier attitude towards administrative forms and recordkeeping. A new staff member, more meticulous by nature, complained about the lack of support she got in trying to organize things in a more orderly way. The staff responded by confronting the new member about being over-conscientious and authoritarian. In a staff meeting it was pointed out that, while this had some truth, the other staff members had anxieties about their own administrative roles which were not being discussed.

(3)   We have now touched on the third use of psychoanalytic concepts, when they are applied to the community as a whole. Psychological interactions may occur between one section of the community and

another, or between the community and outsiders. An example of this is the use of stereotypes: 'the staff don't care', 'the patients avoid taking responsibility', 'the women object to swearing', and so on. Such stereotypes are often associated with 'splitting'. This concept refers to what happens when one group of people (usually called 'we' – e.g. 'we patients', 'we senior staff') is seen as representing good qualities, such as sensitivity and understanding, while the other group ('them') is seen as representing the opposite, lack of understanding, high-handedness, and so forth. This may also arise between the 'we' of the community and the 'them' of people outside, especially people with some influence over the community. Such splits can have a marked effect on personal relationships, since they hinder the appreciation of other people's points of view as individuals. The attempt to understand and examine such collective processes has probably been the most distinctive and original application of psychoanalysis to therapeutic communities, and one that has received a good deal of attention in the literature[1]

PLANNED ENVIRONMENT THERAPY FOR CHILDREN AND ADOLESCENTS

The first attempt to combine psychoanalytic ideas with participative democracy took place in the field of therapeutic education (Bridgeland 1971). At the turn of the twentieth century there were a number of communities for disturbed youngsters in the United States known as Junior Republics. These were mod-elled on the American constitution, with a president, legislative assembly, and so on, all posts being occupied by the young inmates. The rationale behind this was that since the United States was a great nation, the treatment of delinquents in self-governing institutions based on its constitution could not help but suc-ceed. One such 'republic' had been run by a man called Homer Lane, and in 1913 he was invited to England to advise on the setting up of a home for post-schoolage delinquent adolescents.

Although Lane had run a Junior Republic he was rather more psychologi-cally sophisticated in his view of delinquency, seeing it as a product of emo-tional deprivation. His fundamental belief was in the Christian ideal of love, believing in the innate and spontaneous goodness of the child no matter how bad the behaviour. He also possessed considerable charisma and is widely regarded as the most influential pioneer of the principle of self-government for treating disturbed adolescents. Although he was not the first

---

1   There are a number of introductory texts on psychodynamic concepts. Try Brown and Pedder (1991). For an excellent introduction to large group and inter-group processes see Main (1975).

to introduce this principle, he was the first to apply it so completely and so genuinely.

The community he ran was called the Little Commonwealth, and the forty or so adolescent boys and girls and small team of staff were its 'citizens'. Lane wrote:

> The chief point of difference between the Commonwealth and other reformatories is that in the Commonwealth there are no rules and regulations except those made by the boys and girls themselves ... the adult element studiously avoid any assumption of authority in the community except in connection with their duties as teachers or supervisors of labour. [The individual and whole community were free] to make mistakes, to test for themselves the value of every law and the necessity for every restraint imposed upon them. (Quoted in Bridgeland 1971)

An interesting feature of the Little Commonwealth was Lane's 'economic scheme'. The citizens were paid for doing domestic and farm work in the community and were then charged for their lodging, food, clothes, and so forth. If someone had not earned enough to pay for his needs, the other citizens were charged for him. This led to considerable pressure on individuals to behave responsibly towards the community. There was also a Citizens' Court, in which all the members met together to hear complaints about work or conduct and to award punishments. Lane considered that the confrontation of individuals by the group was one of the main forms of therapy in the community.

Psychoanalysis entered into the Little Commonwealth in a rather unfortunate way. While working in England, Lane became enthusiastic about the work of Freud and decided to apply it, perhaps rather recklessly, as a therapeutic technique with some of the girls in his care. There were allegations of sexual impropriety which led to the withdrawal of government support for the school. In 1918 the Little Commonwealth closed. The lesson was learnt by his successors, who with few exceptions did not venture to combine the roles of school head and psychotherapist.

In the 1920s and 1930s a number of pioneer educationalists, some inspired by their contact with Homer Lane, took up the cause of creating liberal therapeutic regimes for delinquent or difficult children. Although they differed in their personal styles, they were all trying to get away from the authoritarian, punitive attitudes of conventional reformatories, and from conventional notions about child–adult relationships in schools generally. One of these pioneers, A.S. Neill, went on to become famous for his many books on liberal education, and for his school, Summerhill, founded in 1924, which still survives, run by his widow. Others created schools in the 1930s which have become legendary in the history of therapeutic work with maladjusted children, among them George Lyward at Finchden Manor, Otto Shaw at Red Hill School, and David Wills at the Hawkspur Camp.

Today these ventures, and many of their successors, are described under the broad heading of Planned Environment Therapy. Despite this different name they have much in common with therapeutic communities. Both stem from a belief in the therapeutic benefits of delegating to the resident or child many of the responsibilities normally taken by staff, in an atmosphere which encourages open expression of feelings and exploration of relationships. Rules and punishments imposed by the staff are rejected in favour of discipline which emerges from the community as a whole, or from the spontaneous relationships between its members.

The man whose work originally gave body to Planned Environment Therapy was David Wills, whose ideas were also probably closest to those of the therapeutic community (Wills 1971). More than other pioneers in this field, his work was of a co-operative nature. His chief collaborator was a doctor, Marjorie Franklin, who through her work in mental hospitals in the 1920s had become interested in the relationship between mental illness and the patients' environment. She wanted to set up special camps for delinquent youths which could demonstrate the benefits of self-government as an educational or therapeutic experience. In 1934 she created a committee of experts to set up and support such 'Q' camps (Q for quest or query), and in David Wills she found the ideal leader for these camps.

Wills, like Tuke, a Quaker, had been inspired by Homer Lane, sharing his belief in the therapeutic value of love and shared responsibility, but not his interest in practising psychoanalytic therapy. The first Q camp was established at Hawkspur Green in 1936, for delinquent boys aged sixteen to nineteen. In addition to Wills who led the camp there was a Selection and Treatment Committee, and the use of outside treatment experts. This ensured that the style and success of the Q camps were not solely dependent on the work of one person, a weakness of many pioneer schools which closed or changed following the leader's death or departure.

Wills's concept of love embraced a number of beliefs: no matter how obnoxious a child's appearance, habits or disposition, he or she is basically good and worthy of love and affection; punishment should never be used to correct or influence a child's behaviour; the domination of one person or group by another is abhorrent – relationships should be egalitarian and non-authoritarian; therapy is based on a loving, accepting relationship being established between a child and one or more adults. The emphasis on egalitarian, non-authoritarian relationships is similar to that in adult therapeutic communities but does not extend to the allocation of roles in the community, where adults still exert certain kinds of traditional authority – for example

matron arranges bedtimes. The emphasis on individual adult–child relationships differs from the emphasis on relationships between residents in most
adult communities.

Wills suggested that there were several advantages of the system of shared
responsibility over conventional authority, some of which betray slightly
mixed motives – for example the fact that adults so seldom give orders tends
to make their authority more effective when they do. Other advantages are
identical with those that apply in adult therapeutic communities: it is a natural vehicle for group therapy, a means by which the children learn that so-
cially acceptable behaviour is demanded of them not only as a result of staff
prejudice but also by their peers, and a way of learning that rules exist for the
mutual protection of individuals. Two other features link Planned Environment Therapy and adult therapeutic communities. One is the therapeutic
value accorded to the work of actually making and servicing the community.
The second is the use of psychoanalytic concepts, especially in handling the
intense relationships between children and staff.

Planned Environment Therapy, although not synonymous with the adult
democratic therapeutic community, resembles it in more ways than it differs
from it. Both recognize the emotional healing power and opportunity for social maturation which can occur when people have jointly to take responsibility for the community they live in. Both emphasize the importance of an
atmosphere of equality and acceptance and the need for essentially non-authoritarian relationships. The difference lies in the separation of specifically
therapeutic relationships, often between the child and a particular adult,
from the more pervasive social learning which takes place in the rest of the
community. In the adult therapeutic community, where the need for a substi-
tute parent may be less pressing, these two aspects of therapy are usually
blended together.

In 1966 the Planned Environment Therapy Trust was formed to promote
the study and use of this form of therapy, which it continues to do through its
Archive and Study Centre founded in 1989. Still in the process of development as a resource for interested professionals, the Study Centre houses a
unique collection of published and unpublished material from pioneer therapeutic communities, which is accessible to the interested student (Fees
1995). More recently the Charterhouse Group was formed to represent
therapeutic communities for children and adolescents in the United
Kingdom (see pages 169–70 for details of these organizations).

CHAPTER 4

Psychiatry Meets World War II

The Hospital as a Therapeutic Community

While democratic and psychoanalytic principles were already being used in therapeutic education, they were introduced quite independently into two psychiatric hospitals during World War II, with far-reaching results. One of these was Northfield military hospital in Birmingham, to which a number of psychoanalysts and social psychologists were posted in the second half of the war. The other was a temporarily converted public school on the outskirts of London, where a young research psychiatrist went to take charge of a unit for patients with psychosomatic anxieties. His name was Maxwell Jones.

Among those who worked at Northfield, three have become widely recognized as the pioneers of this new approach in psychiatry. One was W.R. Bion, who went on to develop his theory of group basic assumptions, arising from work with experiential groups at the Tavistock Clinic, and later to become Britain's most influential post-war contributor to psychoanalytic theory. Another was S.H. Foulkes, who created a method of therapy called group analysis, and later formed the Institute of Group Analysis. The third was Tom Main, who subsequently became the director of the Cassel Hospital, and who first used the term therapeutic community in writing about what went on at Northfield. It was, however, Maxwell Jones, working quite independently at Mill Hill, who was to carry the banner for therapeutic communities after World War II and whose name has been most closely associated with them ever since. Both hospitals have an interesting story to tell, but Northfield's is the more complex.[1]

---

1   In 1996 the journal *Therapeutic Communities* republished the original papers describing the work at Northfield, together with a series of present day commentaries. See Volume 17 Nos. 2 and 3. See also Harrison and Clark (1992).

NORTHFIELD HOSPITAL

W.R. Bion was posted to Northfield early in 1943, at a time when unruly conditions in the hospital required someone with a firm hand. He was put in charge of the training wing – to which patients were moved after their initial four weeks in the hospital wing and before they were posted back to the units or, as many hoped, discharged from active service. When Bion arrived he found things were disorganized. Patients were absent without leave, requesting leave on various pretexts or over-staying the leave they had, while the officers were uncertain what their duties were supposed to be. 'What was required', he wrote, 'was the sort of discipline achieved in a theatre of war by an experienced officer in command of a rather scallywag battalion. But what sort of discipline is that?' He decided to regard discipline not just as his problem but as a communal problem, to make it the common enemy to be studied and tackled by the entire training wing of about one hundred men, as they would study an outside enemy (Bion 1961).

In order to try to bring about such a remarkable shift in the patients' attitudes he announced a framework of various activities in which he expected the men to take part. He also instituted a daily 'parade' of thirty minutes for the men to step outside this framework and look at its working. The men were free to react as they chose but would have their behaviour noted. This freedom, he calculated, would provide an opportunity for them to show their true aims, while the framework would provide something against which the unruliness and indiscipline of individuals could be highlighted and discussed. He refused, at least outwardly, to have the cure for discipline made his responsibility. When some of the men complained that others were shirking he attempted to use this as a starting point for discussion of the problem. He found that his determination produced, after a vivid and healthy impatience, a real belief that the unit was meant to tackle its job with scientific seriousness ... within a month of the inception of the scheme, changes had taken place. Whereas at first it seemed difficult to find ways of employing the men, at the end of the month it was difficult to find time for the work they wanted to do.

Despite its success, the experiment ended after six weeks. Recounting it some years later Tom Main said, 'Neither the commanding officer nor his staff was able to tolerate the early weeks of chaos, and both were condemning and rancorous about Bion's refusal to own total responsibility for the disorder of others'. The upshot was that both Bion and the commanding officer were removed when their rows came to the notice of higher authority. Here ended the first lesson which, according to Main, was that Bion 'had failed to work at and get and maintain social sanction for his deeds ... he had been therapeutic for his ward but antitherapeutic for the military staff' (Main 1977).

Bion left Northfield in May 1943. He had been there for three months. Two months later Foulkes – a psychoanalyst who was at that time pioneering small group therapy with his private patients – was appointed as a senior psychiatrist in charge of one of the wards on the hospital wing. Clearly, the aftermath of Bion's departure was still evident, for although Foulkes knew nothing of Bion's experiment when he arrived at Northfield, he found that the training wing (which Bion had run) was now run by military training officers and the psychiatrists were expected to limit their activities to the hospital wing. Foulkes was at Northfield from 1943 till 1946, and was able to chart in detail what he later called the 'second experiment' in creating a therapeutic community – this time more slowly and more securely sanctioned (Foulkes 1948,1964). He outlined four phases:

Phase 1

The hospital was rigidly divided into different sections with little co-ordination between them or between the medical staff. It was a forbidding and uncomfortable place, and new patients 'soon found their way, not to their duties but to Jones's cafe nearby'. In other words it was a typical large institution with two cultures: the official one imposed by the staff, and the unofficial one to which the patients looked for support and information. During this phase Foulkes treated only his own ward patients in groups.

Phase 2

After a year the administrators appeared to lose some of their suspicion of psychiatrists, who were allowed to continue their involvement with patients when they were transferred to the training wing. Co-ordination between the medical staff improved, the nurses became more actively involved in decision making, and barriers between staff throughout the hospital began to fall. Foulkes extended his groups, using new techniques such as psychodrama (he knew of Moreno's work) and teaching interested staff and visitors about groups. As yet patients were not involved in running any hospital activities.

Phase 3

After about six months came the real beginnings of a therapeutic community. It coincided with the arrival of several new staff with an interest in group psychology. Among them were Harold Bridger, an enthusiastic exponent of leaderless small groups, and a new lieutenant colonel to whom Foulkes would be responsible, Tom Main. Both Foulkes and Main saw as their task the furthering of the group treatment of patients, although there were tensions between them in the way they approached this task. Foulkes' main interest was in the individuals he treated in his groups while Main focused on the wider system. In an interview some years later he was critical of Foulkes and others who 'wanted to go on treating people ... when there were bloody great issues to be solved' (Harrison and Clark 1992). Aided by Bridger's enthusiasm, not only therapy groups but also patient-organized group projects began to flourish. The training wing became transformed into an organization for promoting activities of all sorts. Hobby groups formed, a newspaper group, a chess group, a drama group, a printing group, a typing group, and so on. Foulkes described the therapeutic value of this as follows:

> As far as possible the patients' activities were organised and maintained by the patients themselves; if they failed in their responsibility they carried the onus and shared the disability; if the (patient) band did not turn up for the dance there was no dance, but if they succeeded they had their own reward – the result was that above all they became active on their own behalf and used the hospital for their own benefit instead of waiting for good to be done to them. (Foulkes 1948, pp.51–2)

In contrast with the split cultures in Phase 1 there was now one culture in which the patients and staff were both involved. Patients shared in hospital management, and there was contact between patients, nurses, doctors, and other staff in the meetings and common work in which they were all engaged. The extent of these changes brought their own problems. 'Because the groups contained human beings,' wrote Main, 'troubles abounded, inefficiency, quarrels, arguments, sulks and walkouts occurred'. Foulkes became a kind of troubleshooter, going to wherever a crisis had arisen, to work out with the group what the problem was and how best to resolve it. Yet the final hurdle in the experiment lay not with the patients but with the hospital as a whole.

Phase 4

Morale in the hospital was beginning to sag and spontaneity was diminishing once more. Various causes for this were diagnosed. Foulkes saw it as a problem of what had been new and fresh becoming institutionalized. New patients arriving felt as though the system was imposed on them, just as it had been in Phase 1. The solution he saw was to start off a new round of patient-organized activities which would once more bring everyone into spontaneous and productive contact, to 'get the hospital as a whole again to play as a concerted orchestra' (Foulkes 1948).

Main's solution lay on a different level. He identified problems among the staff as the underlying malaise. It has since become a well-established part of therapeutic community practice that staff should have regular meetings to discuss difficulties in their relationships, yet the reasons for this are not always appreciated. Much later, Main looked back at this period and described how his ideas took shape at that time. I think his account conveys a sense of discovery that makes it worth quoting at length:

> Northfield was now, by 1946, a hospital of a new kind, in which both patients and therapeutic staff sought to explore in a way never attempted before the unconscious tensions which pain the lives of individuals and of the small groups they find themselves living in. It looked – as Foulkes teased me – highly chaotic, but both hospital divisions were in fact busy, efficient and relatively free from unresolvable internal tensions. It was also innovative and exciting. Yet in the larger hospital there were strains. Something was not quite right.
>
> In the larger community many of the non-therapeutic military staff, administrative, domestic, maintenance and to a lesser extent secretarial, were of low morale. Some openly resented patients taking the right of action or decision over matters of work or equipment and it was true that patients would organise group discussions and activities which regularly overlapped or contradicted or interfered with the military staff's wishes, duties or expectations. The staff were being ignored and after all they, not the patients, were there to run things. Treatment was treatment: fair enough; patients should be treated kindly because they were ill but they should do what they were told; when things went wrong staff should step in and correct things and show the way; it should not be left to patients to sort out troubles; things had gone too far; it was the psychiatrists.
>
> My commanding officer made it plain that his tolerance was now at an end, and I began to think about Bion's fate. I had resolved however not to share it, however noble that would be, and wondered how to preserve the tottering sanctions for our work. I tried not to feel either too guilty or too righteous and wronged – without greet success – and to free myself to think about my commanding officer's plight. Why could he not control his staff and support our work? Why had this otherwise pleasant, intelligent man become regularly stupid, angry and threatening? Why did he feel himself threatened by events? With some difficulty I ceased to be so self-centred and began to see that he had troubles of his own. He was responsible to his seniors and he was also the inevitable repository for all the grumbles and discontents of his military, administrative and artisan staff which I and others, safe in our military rank and medical authority, had ignored or brushed aside as reactionary. Yet he was being fed by his military juniors with these discontents as the head of the administrative and domestic hierarchy of the hospital which was separate and distinct from the therapeutic hierarchy which I represented.

I then realised that the almost daily rows he and I conducted were about unresolved tensions, not between him and me as individuals but between the lower-order systems of military and therapeutic staff fed upwards and into us. These tensions had been regarded as nuisances, issues not for open study or scientific scrutiny but for noisy argument or silent power struggles. He and I were being unconsciously required by our own staffs to be their champions and to conduct these struggles on their behalf; and we had been unconscious of this. So now there was a new set of problems. How to ensure that the tensions could be examined, perhaps resolved, where they began – between people in the lower hospital systems? How to put the lower-order military staff in touch with the needs of the lower-order therapeutic staff and patients? And vice versa. What were the unconscious fantasies each system grew about the other? How much blind mutual projection of evil was going on and distorting perceptions of each other?

One evening I suddenly realised the whole community, all staff as well as all patients, needed to be viewed as a troubled larger system which needed treatment. Could all people in it move to consideration of other people's plight, and benefit from opportunities to examine the conscious and unconscious uses each was making of others? Could the total institution become therapeutic for all? Clearly we would need a total culture of enquiry if we were regularly to examine, understand and perhaps resolve the tensions and defensive use of roles which are inevitable in any total system. Today the concept is well-worn, and the term I coined for it – the Therapeutic Community – is now in use so widespread that the coinage is somewhat debased; but then it was new and for me at least it was a sudden insight, a major conceptual shift, a new way of viewing events in a hospital. It also demanded appropriate viewing instruments. At this level of system – a whole community – techniques of investigation and intervention had yet to be devised; indeed today argument about them still seems wholly proper. But now at Northfield inter-staff relations and staff–patient relations began to be seen as legitimate matters for regular, indeed essential, study whereas hitherto only patient–staff, patient–doctor and patient interrelations had been. This attempt to create an atmosphere of respect for all and the examination of all difficulties would be a long way from the medical model, whereby disease is skillfully treated in anonymous people under blanket medical compassion and served by a clinically aloof and separate administration. (Main 1977)

It may be helpful to summarize the key ideas which were developed at Northfield by Bion, Foulkes and Main.

(1)   The problem of disruptive behaviour in the ward is defined as a shared, common problem rather than the leader's problem. Bion identifies it as the 'common enemy to be studied and attacked'. (This was a particularly apt metaphor in wartime.)

(2)   A clear programme of events, activities, etc., is set up through which patients are free to move as they choose rather than having an agenda imposed on them. In this way individuals' true intentions are revealed, to be contrasted with their professed ones. Their behaviour and responses are then reviewed in regular meetings at which attendance is required.

(3)   Groups are set up with various tasks to perform. This leads the members to have mutual expectations of one another and to communicate and co-operate with others. Foulkes sees the activity itself as secondary, from a therapeutic point of view, to the social interactions it fosters.

(4)   Leadership is used not as an end in itself but as a stepping stone towards patients taking it over themselves. Leadership needs first to be securely established by staff and then given up as patients grow to assume it themselves.

(5)   A 'culture of enquiry' is established, to use Tom Main's phrase. This especially includes the relationships between the staff, whose frustrations are otherwise directed towards heads of department who get into repetitive conflicts with one another.

(6)   It is recognized that innovation in one part of an organization always affects other parts, and that it is vital to work with all the affected parts of the organization if the innovation is not to be attacked by them.

(7)   The term therapeutic community is used by Main as a general label for these new ideas.

MILL HILL HOSPITAL

In contrast to Northfield, there were no special problems of low morale, unruly behaviour, or conflict amongst the staff at Mill Hill when Maxwell Jones arrived there in 1940. Part of London's Maudsley Hospital had been evacuated there at the outbreak of war and the unit of which he was in charge had been set up to study what was known as effort syndrome.[2] This was a condition in which physical exercise caused people to become breathless and giddy, and to suffer from palpitations and chest pains. Such patients were often convinced that they

2   See Jones (1968) and Jones (1979) for Maxwell Jones' own account of this period.

had a serious heart disease. This was a prevalent condition in wartime and during the six years he was there over two thousand patients passed through the unit.

At this stage in his career Jones was primarily interested in physiological research, and had only a passing and sceptical interest in psychoanalysis. For the first two years, he conducted numerous experiments designed to determine the precise nature and causes of effort syndrome. He was a good researcher, and his thesis describing this work won him a gold medal from Edinburgh University. He was also an open-minded and practical scientist. Having determined the physiological mechanisms which underlay effort syndrome, he reasoned that if these patients could understand for themselves how their symptoms were caused, they might stop worrying about their hearts. His aim was not to cure them but to change their attitudes, to enable them to recognize that they had a minor disability rather than a major illness.

In 1941 he decided to introduce a series of lectures to educate the patients about human physiology. Three times a week one hundred men gathered to listen and discuss their symptoms. Then an unexpected thing began to happen. Patients who had already completed the 'course' of lectures and had not yet left the hospital began to help by explaining things to the newcomers, and became enthusiastic and unexpectedly articulate in doing so.

Jones was not slow to recognize the beneficial effects of patients helping one another in this way; it brought out what was 'well' and healthy in them, increasing morale and self-esteem. From this beginning the unit gradually moved towards patients taking a more equal role with the staff in other activities. This was helped by the fact that the nurses were mostly conscripts who, lacking traditional training in nurse–patient relationships, were happy to change towards a more democratic way of working.

As this approach evolved over the next four years, so its application widened beyond changing the attitude of patients towards their symptoms. Later, Jones wrote that it soon became apparent that the patients' reactions in the hospital 'were similar to their reactions outside, and the study of these real life situations (in the hospital) gave a great deal of information about the patient's problems'. It was in order to make the most use of this new approach that he evolved a new hospital structure which included 'more open communication; less rigid hierarchy of doctors, nurses, patients; daily structured discussions of the whole unit, and various sub-groups' (Jones 1968).

Thus Jones evolved an approach which began to look increasingly like the one at Northfield. Although less dramatic than events at that hospital, developments at Mill Hill were in their own way just as remarkable, perhaps even more so given Jones' lack of prior acquaintance with group techniques. The convergence of psychiatrists with quite different backgrounds – psychoanalysis and physiological research on the idea of using the *way a hospital was run* as the medium for therapy – was a sign that a basic shift in psychiatric thinking was in the making. Psychiatry had met World War II and made creative use of the encounter.

CHAPTER 5

From Innovation to Application

Therapeutic Communities for People with Severe Personality Disorders

The terms psychopath and, more recently, severe personality disorder have generated considerable debate over the question of whether people labelled in this way can in fact be treated, or whether the condition is untreatable. A brief clarification of terms is given at the end of this chapter but it is beyond the scope of the book to enter into the full debate. However therapeutic community practitioners have always been on the side of those who believe such people can be helped to change, and more recently there has been support for this view from empirical studies (Cullen 1994, Dolan *et al.* 1996) and from Government reviews (Reed 1994). In this chapter we look at the development of therapeutic communities whose target population was people with personality disorders, although these communities were later used as inspiration for work with quite different populations. We also look at the development of therapeutic communities in prisons, designed to help those offenders who want to change their antisocial patterns of behaviour.

MAXWELL JONES AND THE HENDERSON HOSPITAL

Although it was Tom Main who coined the term therapeutic community, it was Maxwell Jones whose name came to be most closely identified with the therapeutic community movement. The ideas and methods which most mental health workers refer to when they speak of a therapeutic community are those developed by Maxwell Jones, his colleagues and successors, at the unit which since 1958 has been called Henderson Hospital, or simply the Henderson.[1] Although the idea of an orthodox therapeutic community is unhelpful, antithetical to the vital culture of enquiry, the Henderson has undoubtedly provided inspiration for many treatment centres around the world that have borrowed from and adapted its methods.

---

1 This account draws on Jones (1968) and Whiteley (1980). Quotations are from Jones (1968).

Following the experiments of World War II, Jones wanted to continue his interest in the way hospitals were organized, and his clinical interest shifted from patients with psychosomatic symptoms to those whose problems were primarily social and interpersonal. For a year he ran a transitional community, rehabilitating emotionally disturbed prisoners-of-war returning to Britain after many years in prison camps. In 1947 he became the director of a new unit set up to tackle the problem of unemployed 'drifters', at Belmont Hospital in Surrey. Initially this was called the Industrial Neurosis Unit, later the Social Rehabilitation Unit, and in 1958, coinciding with Jones' own departure to America, it was renamed Henderson Hospital. It was and remains probably the best known of all hospital-based therapeutic communities, specializing in the treatment of people with severe personality disorders.

At Belmont, Jones and his colleagues developed a number of procedures and principles which could be readily applied by others. If Bion, Foulkes and Main had created a feast of new ideas at Northfield, it was Jones who sat down and produced a recipe that others could follow. Three of the key ingredients are community meetings, staff review meetings, and 'living learning' situations.

At a daily community meeting all the staff and patients meet in a large circle to discuss what has been going on in the community over the past twenty-four hours and to examine any problems that have come up. This is the focus or hub of the community, into which events in other group meetings and activities are fed back, and in which decisions and ideas are debated, with the staff not necessarily taking a leading role. Such meetings can have various aims, as discussed in Chapter 1. For Jones, two aims were central. Taking a responsible part in the affairs of the community helps patients to overcome their lack of confidence and low self-esteem, and through discussion of particular incidents patients can learn what feelings and perceptions lie behind behaviour, testing distorted perceptions against the common consensus.

Immediately following each community meeting there is a staff review meeting in which the interactions in the community meeting are discussed. This is particularly important for examining the relationships between staff, and to enable staff who may be new to this way of working to express and deal with the anxiety and frustration they will almost certainly feel at the change from more conventional staff roles. The overlap of responsibilities between staff in different disciplines and between staff and residents mean that clarification is continually needed concerning who takes responsibility for what. To take an example, in a conventionally run hospital ward everyone considers it the nurses' responsibility to see that the ward is kept clean and tidy. In a therapeutic community this is often regarded as the patients' responsibility. Nurses new to this method may find this difficult to accept and may need to discuss their feelings about this change in their role. Similarly doctors, used to being the main decision makers, may find it hard to share decisions with the rest of the staff and the patients. The staff review session provides an opportunity for newcomers to learn and for all staff to sort out problems inherent in the relationships between different disciplines.

One of the terms Jones is best known for is the living learning situation. When a crisis occurs involving all or some members of the community, rather than wait for the next community meeting, a crisis meeting can immediately be called of all the people concerned in the crisis. Jones describes this as a

> face-to-face confrontation and joint analysis of the current interpersonal difficulty. Each individual is helped to become more aware of the thinking and the feeling of the others and this leads to a more comprehensive view of the situation as it affects each of the people involved ... frequent exposure to situations of this kind if handled skillfully can contribute to personal growth and maturation

Other ingredients evolved by Jones and the Henderson staff included work groups followed by discussion between the members about their responses during the work; role-play of situations outside hospital which residents may have to face; and a selection committee for new patients which is made up of staff and residents in equal proportion, with equal voting rights.

In addition a wide range of posts were created to which residents could be elected, for example work co-ordinator, ward representative, chairman. There were also two terms which have entered into the daily vocabulary of mental health work – role blurring and feedback. Role blurring is itself a rather blurred term. It was originally used to refer to the overlap or flexibility of roles which occurred in therapeutic communities, where a nurse could do a job normally carried out by a social worker, or a doctor could do something normally done by a nurse, and so on. This could naturally create some confusion without frequent staff discussions, and today role blurring is often used to refer to the situation where roles are not properly defined and people are uncertain about their role. Role blurring need not lead to role confusion if sufficient discussion takes place about who is doing what.

Feedback usually refers to the practice of reporting back in a meeting something of therapeutic importance that happened elsewhere. A conversation between two people may be fed back to a group, or events in small group meetings may be fed back into the community meeting. This is done in the belief that community members are in the best position to understand and help one another if they are fully informed about each other's feelings and behaviour. This may appear to breach the ethics of confidentiality, but since it is the community as a whole that treats the patient rather than the doctor,

le of confidentiality now extends to the whole community. In
this may be difficult for some newcomers to accept, and the amount
ail contained in a feedback may need to be modified according to the
vel of trust which has been built up between community members.

In addition to Jones' own work, in the 1950s he invited a team of sociologists led by Robert Rapoport to study the Social Rehabilitation Unit (as it was then called). The result was an important book, *Community as Doctor*, published in 1960. Among the team's findings was the occurrence of a repeated cycle of oscillations within the community. At certain times residents were able to take a lot of responsibility and the unit ran quite democratically. There then occurred a series of disturbances which escalated to the point where the staff needed to play a more active role for a while, until residents once more became involved in the running of the community. The account of these oscillations has been of great relevance to other communities where similar cycles have been noticed. The book also highlighted a conflict between those staff who were mainly interested in preparing residents for the outside world, and those who focused on what was going on within the community and on helping residents to understand themselves better. This was conceptualized as a conflict between the goals of rehabilitation and treatment. Again this has been found in many other communities.

The most widely known finding in Rapoport's work was the result of a questionnaire dealing with the values that the staff held about treatment. Four principles emerged which have since become synonymous with therapeutic communities of the democratic analytic type:

(1)   'Democratization': every member of the community (i.e. all
       residents/patients/clients and staff) should share equally in the
       exercise of power in decision making about community affairs.

(2)   'Permissiveness': all members should tolerate from one another a wide
       degree of behaviour that might be distressing or seem deviant by
       ordinary standards.

(3)   'Communalism': there should be tight-knit, intimate sets of
       relationships, with sharing of amenities (dining room, etc.), use of first
       names, and free communication.

(4)   'Reality confrontation': patients should be continuously presented
       with interpretations of their behaviour as it is seen by others, in order
       to counteract their tendency to distort, deny or withdraw from their
       difficulties in getting on with others.

There is some discrepancy between these values, shared by the staff, and Maxwell Jones' own views. For example, Jones saw democracy as giving residents 'that degree of responsibility which is compatible with their capacity at any one time'. The difference between this and the 'equal exercise of power' is the difference between seeing the therapeutic community as a method of treatment to be used at the discretion of the therapist, and seeing it as an ideology concerned with the abolition of inequality between different classes – in this case residents and staff. The practical consequences of these two views may often be the same, at least when the community is in the democratic phase of its oscillations. At other times disagreements may develop between those who see democracy in ideological or therapeutic terms.

It is useful to realize that the principles of permissiveness and reality confrontation go together: patients can do what they like but whatever they do will be a matter for confrontation and discussion if it interferes with their relationships with others. This combination of permissiveness with confrontation and interpretation is central to all therapies based directly or indirectly on psychoanalysis. It links the Henderson with Bion's attempt to get his men to study their own disorderly behaviour, and with the refusal of the pioneer educationalists to impose adult authority on maladjusted children. In 1997 Henderson Hospital celebrated its fiftieth anniversary. It continues to function as a therapeutic community of the democratic analytic type, and also as a centre for visits and training courses.

TOM MAIN AND THE CASSEL HOSPITAL

The Cassel Hospital began as a small, private hospital for neurotic disorders in 1919 and gradually developed a psychoanalytic orientation. In 1946 Tom Main moved from Northfield to become its new director, a post which he held for thirty years. In 1948 this was the only psychiatric hospital in the new Naional Health Service where all the doctors were trained or training in psychoanalysis. It might have continued as an in-patient psychotherapy hospital for neurosis but under Main's influence there evolved a unique system, combining a therapeutic community in which nurses and patients participated as equals, with individual or group psychotherapy which took place between the patients and the doctors. In this model there was a quite deliberate separation between the 'outer' world of social roles, work tasks and current relationships, and the 'inner' world of private fantasy and feelings. Here the conflict between the goals of treatment and rehabilitation which had troubled the Henderson staff was resolved by creating two parallel systems of therapy.

The role of the nurse was of particular interest. It was considered important that she should be regarded not as a second-rate psychotherapist but as a professional with a role distinct from the doctor's. This role was given the name 'psychosocial nursing'. The Cassel has become a major centre for post-graduate training of nurses in this specialized type of work and has produced a number of books about it (Barnes 1968, Barnes et al. 1998). In psychosocial nursing the main task is to help the community and its members to 'get on with the work and maintain adult roles'. Nurses work *with* the patients rather than for them, as equal, responsible citizens (the same term that Homer Lane used to describe the members of the Little Commonwealth). 'Each group, with an elected manager, is responsible for maintaining, cleaning and decorating a particular area of the hospital, and for managing its own work programme.' The nurse may help the members to learn from their behaviour, but prevents the group becoming preoccupied with therapeutic problems that distract from the tasks in hand.

This division of the doctors' and the nurses' roles contrasts with the principle of role blurring between staff, and of blending practical and therapeutic tasks, which is characteristic of most therapeutic communities developed in hospital settings. It presents an alternative use of the principle of democratization within an overall structure in which staff take specialized therapeutic roles. Although this may seem, from an ideological point of view, to be opposed to the therapeutic community ethic, from a therapeutic point of view such a structure may be an equally effective way of helping psychologically disorganized and self-destructive patients to gain a sense of control over their feelings and experience. The relative effectiveness of these two models is an empirical question that has still to be addressed in a systematic way, although evaluation of the models separately has shown encouraging results (Dolan *et al.* 1996, Chiesa 1997).

The model used by the Cassel is one where an external structure provides a sense of order which the patient is gradually able to internalize – i.e. learn to apply to themselves. It is an approach similar to the one used by some pioneers of therapeutic education, and also resembles that of the concept-based therapeutic communities to be described later.

DAY HOSPITALS

Communities are places where people live and, by and large, therapeutic communities are too. However, the methods of the therapeutic community can be applied in day settings, provided enough time is spent together and enough activities are shared to create a sense of community. The first day hospital for psychiatric patients was the Marlborough Day Hospital in London, set up by Joshua Bierer in 1946. This was part of a comprehensive scheme for helping patients to be independent of full-time hospital treatment. This hospital later evolved into a therapeutic community using a wide variety of different group therapy techniques and with considerable involvement of patients in the way the community was organized. Although a combination of staff difficulties and external pressures led to its closure in 1977, a lasting legacy has been the excellent guide *What Happens in Groups* by Bob Hinshelwood (1987) based on his experiences there.

In recent years the move away from in-patient treatment has encouraged a number of innovations. One of the most significant has been by the Winter-bourne Unit, first established as an in-patient unit at Fair Mile Hospital in 1970, and then evolving in the 1980s into a five-days-a-week day unit, eventually moving to a city centre location in Reading in the early 1990s (Knowles 1995). The Unit is able to work with people with the kind of personality disorders that would usually require the containment of in-patient treatment on a five-days-per-week basis. It does this through a combination of the usual therapeutic ingredients of meetings and shared responsibilities, together with a carefully managed mutual support network comprising a system of telephone contact and, if necessary, of meetings between members outside community hours of 9a.m. and 3.30p.m. (Higgins 1997). This provides members with the experience of feeling emotionally contained when they are not at the Unit. The principle that it is not for social calls but for members to use on their own behalf when requiring support is respected and has rarely been abused.

THERAPEUTIC COMMUNITIES FOR OFFENDERS

A prison might be the last place you would expect to find a therapeutic community. Prisons have traditionally been for taking away people's freedom, imposing rigid discipline and limiting their opportunity for social involvement. Yet there have been a number of experiments aimed at making prisons therapeutic. Some of these were limited to the introduction of individual or group counselling, or to improving the environment and relaxing the formality. In the 1960s two attempts were made to run part or all of a prison as a therapeutic community on the lines of the Henderson: one at Chino in California, the other at Grendon Underwood in Buckinghamshire, England.

At Chino a project was undertaken by Dennie Briggs, a clinical psychologist, to create a therapeutic community for fifty of the prisoners, who volunteered for the project. An initial year was allowed for training staff, working out group procedures and starting, with a small group of enthusiastic volunteers, to create a 'culture' that would influence the main group when they came. The programme included regular community meetings, small psychotherapy groups and work groups. There was a good deal of apprehensiveness to begin with.

> We needed to know how convicted felons in prison would take to a culture which required 'feedback' to operate. Would they see this as 'snitching'? Would they be able to violate the well established 'inmate code of ethics' and feed incidences of delinquent behaviour publicly into

the meetings? If men were encouraged to talk openly about their current anxieties at being in prison, would their feelings erupt and get out of control? Could you contain anger and hostility in large groups? What would happen to staff control if inmates talked too freely?

Early large group meetings were viewed with considerable anxiety by the custodial officials. The first meeting with over twenty men was a cautious experience. Extra custodial officials were stationed nearby in case anger erupted and became unmanageable. (Briggs 1972, p.118)

No ill-effects resulted, and the staff and inmates began to relax. Despite this, prison officers were reluctant to become involved in the discussions as they believed that open confrontation would jeopardize their authority. Particular problems arose over the work arrangements in the prison laundry. This serviced the whole prison and a number of 'rackets' were being operated there, common to institutions with an active 'underlife', which clashed with the values of the project. There was also the same kind of conflict as Tom Main had described at Northfield, between the custodial and therapeutic staff. The former expected delinquent behaviour, if found out, to be punished, while the latter were against taking disciplinary action.

As more delinquent activities were reported and no action taken, custodial officials in the institution became more alarmed and viewed the project as a place fostering delinquency rather than controlling and punishing it. (Briggs 1972, p.127)

The future of the project seemed at risk, when a more serious crisis involving the whole prison proved to be its salvation. An incident between a white member of the project and a black inmate not in the project had created an explosive situation which seemed destined to escalate into a race riot. Prisoners and staff were both amassing weapons in readiness. A crisis meeting of staff and inmates was called in the therapeutic community and an open sharing of staff frustration led to an effort to work together to avert the riot. The anticipated riot did not take place and the project at last won the confidence of the prison authorities.

Developments at Grendon Underwood were different since the whole prison was designed to function as a collection of wings each run as a separate therapeutic community (Gunn et al. 1978). It was built as a unique experiment within the English prison system and remains the only one of its kind, although smaller therapeutic communities have been set up at Wormwood Scrubs, Gartree and Barlinnie in Glasgow (Cullen et al. 1997). As at Chino, attention was paid at Grendon to establishing the right atmosphere. Care was taken to avoid creating a prison subculture by taking men, who all came from other prisons, only a few at a time. A total of about two hundred prisoners were to be catered for, most of them in their teens and twenties, within a year or so from their release.

One of the main effects of running the prison as a therapeutic community was to break down the traditional roles which prisoners and officers created for themselves and each other, as enshrined in the terms 'cons' and 'screws'. Prisoners were able to give up the need to impress their peers. One said

> Here you have the freedom to drop any fronts, to be yourself. You don't have to live a lie. You don't have to pretend to a big time gangster. Here I can say I'm a petty thief. And sex cases don't have to cower in the corner.

The effect could be as marked for officers as for inmates, as it was for one tough disciplinarian who was transferred to Grendon against his wishes. He was wholly out of sympathy with the system, and refused to attend wing meetings on the grounds that he had no wish to hear what inmates had to say. Over a period of time his attitude changed. Asked to describe what happened, he said, 'At X [the prison he'd come from] they were all cons. Here they're blokes.'

In the 1970s a major study was undertaken to evaluate what effects Grendon had. It found that inmates left prison feeling less anxious and depressed, more self-confident, better able to relate to people and less hostile towards society. However studies of reconviction in the 1970s found that overall rates of reoffending were not significantly reduced. More recent studies have looked at the length of time prisoners remained in therapy at Grendon and found that the longer the term in therapy the lower the rate of reconviction. Only one in five of the men who stay more than eighteen months are reconvicted within two years – a fairly remarkable result. Despite this there is uncertainty over the future of Grendon as a therapeutic prison in the wake of government demands for increased security and cuts in expenditure throughout the English prison system (Cullen 1997).

Grendon's success has generated considerable interest in the application of therapeutic community methods in prisons in Britain. Although the Special Unit at Barlinnie was closed in 1994, the general trend appears to be towards an increased acceptance of well-run therapeutic communities for particular types of prisoner – young men who have committed serious offences and have an interest in learning how to change their maladaptive responses. One sign of this trend has been the formation of a prison section within the Association of Therapeutic Communities. Another is the decision by the British Home Office to commission a second Grendon-style prison in 1998.

While tentative progress is taking place in the prison system in the United Kingdom, therapeutic communities of the concept-based type (described in Chapter 7) have become the 'treatment of choice' in American prisons where drug abusers make up a large proportion of the prison population (Wexler 1997).

A NOTE ON THE TERM PERSONALITY DISORDER

Different kinds of personality disorder are now recognized. Severe personality disorder is associated with the kind of repeated antisocial behaviour and lack of empathy that used to be associated with the term psychopath, and it is this type of personality disorder that therapeutic communities have proved effective in treating (Dolan *et al.* 1996). The term borderline personality disorder is associated with individuals who demonstrate both destructive behaviour, often towards themselves, and symptoms more usually associated with psychosis-like delusions and hallucinations. The 'borderline' refers to the borderline between these two types of disorder. While the term borderline personality disorder has been in use for some time in the United States it is only now beginning to be used much in the United Kingdom. Patients who present the combination of problems covered by this term have often been the victim of physical or sexual abuse in childhood, and require a special kind of treatment environment that combines firm but non-punitive management with great sensitivity and understanding. Some therapeutic communities such as the Cassel have for many years worked with such patients. Over the last few years new therapeutic models have been developed which more explicitly combine therapeutic community principles with principles derived from work on the effects of traumatic stress (Bloom 1997, Croese 1997). Other therapeutic communities are beginning to draw on cognitive behavioural approaches such as Dialectical Behaviour Therapy (Linehan 1993). This seems to be an area of clinical activity where those who work with different therapeutic models are collaborating in interesting and potentially creative ways.

CHAPTER 6

The Therapeutic Community Approach in the Care of the Mentally Ill

We have seen that communities based on the principles of democratic participation and psychoanalytic understanding were first created for maladjusted children in the early part of the twentieth century. Later these same principles were applied in psychiatric units specializing in the treatment of neurotic or personality disorders, and the term therapeutic community was coined. The principles and methods discovered and elaborated in these places have subsequently been taken up, modified, and applied in a wide range of settings in many countries for people with mental disorders.

The extent of these developments has varied between countries and over time in ways that are difficult to explain. Factors likely to influence this process include the attitudes of mental health professionals, changes in the wider political and economic climate, and the stage of evolution of mental health services in the country in question. It has been argued that therapeutic communities are more likely to be established where there is a certain liberalization in progress in the political climate with a questioning of conventional forms of medical and social work practice (Clark 1977) or when a major social upheaval dissolves conventional social roles and creates a space for new ideas and relationships (Kennard 1991). There is a curious phenomenon by which therapeutic communities can be seen as 'old hat' in one country or service at the same time as being seen as pioneering and innovative in another. For example, in England therapeutic communities have been *passé* in general psychiatry from the mid-1970s onwards, but in the 1990s have been seen as increasingly relevant in prisons, secure settings and in the voluntary sector. Meanwhile there has been a move away from therapeutic communities in some countries – for example Holland – but a growth in the number of therapeutic communities in others – for example in Italy following its mental hospital closure programme of the 1980s.

THE MOVE FROM HOSPITAL TO COMMUNITY CARE

In 1948 the newly created National Health Service took over responsibility for all the one hundred or so local authority mental hospitals (the county asylums) in the United Kingdom. Many were filled with patients who had been admitted to hospital as young adults and were now in their forties, fifties or older, having remained there ever since. Conditions in these hospitals were often dreadful, as described in Chapter 2. Up to a hundred patients could be living in barely furnished wards with few personal possessions, regimented clothes and haircuts, and little to do all day. In the 1950s some of these hospitals began to introduce methods which blended the old principles of moral treatment and the new therapeutic community ideas. Group meetings, patient responsibilities, a belief in the value of purposeful activity were some of the common features of these hospitals. The goal was not to 'cure' the patients nor necessarily to rehabilitate them back into the wider community, although resettlement with a degree of continuing support might be a realistic aim for some. To a greater extent the therapeutic community approach was about restoring to patients a more normal pattern of daily living, helping them learn how to communicate and get on with the people they lived with.

David Clark, who pioneered this way of working as medical superintendent of Fulbourn Hospital in Cambridge in the 1950s and 1960s, called it the 'therapeutic community approach' to distinguish it from the 'therapeutic community proper' of specialized units like the Henderson and the Cassel. Compared to the bleak and pointless existence of patients in these hospitals before 1948 it was very successful. In a number of the large English mental hospitals, such as Fulbourn, Littlemore in Oxford and Claybury in north London, patients who had languished in back wards for decades began attending ward meetings and other activities and were able to come and go from wards that had previously been kept locked. Some were able to progress towards sheltered employment and living outside hospital in staffed hostels or group homes. In the 1960s and 1970s these hospitals were recognized as centres of excellence in the rehabilitation of the chronic mentally ill. Yet ironically their success was also their swansong. Those long-term patients who could leave hospital did so but those who remained in hospital were less responsive to a therapeutic community approach. Hospitals such as Littlemore and Fulbourn turned to creating therapeutic communities for new psychiatric admissions, but in the 1970s the political programme of reform was beginning to take effect to close many of the old asylums. The intention was to achieve the twin goals of overcoming the segregation of mentally ill people from the communities they came from, and hoped-for financial savngs. In the event good quality community care has proved no cheaper than hospital care and there still remains a recognized need for residential care for those severely mentally ill people who are either dangerous, difficult to place or acutely disturbed (Leff 1997).

In pursuing this policy much of the progress made in the large mental hospitals, together with the collective knowledge and commitment of professional teams, has been lost to the field of psychiatry. In theory the therapeutic community know-how of the mental hospitals could be relocated into the community. In practice this transfer has been patchy and probably more relevant in the voluntary sector.

THE MODIFIED THERAPEUTIC COMMUNITY FOR THE CHRONIC MENTALLY ILL

One of the hallmarks of all therapeutic communities is a breaking down of the splits between staff and patient roles that characterize more traditional settings, giving patients responsibilities of various kinds: for practical tasks in the community, for therapeutic support, for some of the decisions affecting the community. In working with people suffering from chronic and severe mental illness the delegation to patients of these responsibilities is real but limited. The goals are still determined largely by staff, at least in the early stages of treatment, and staff focus a lot of thought on getting the balance right between not being too democratic and not being too controlling. Neither extreme is therapeutic. If goals are determined democratically many patients would choose to retain the institutional pattern of living to which they had become accustomed, afraid of trying anything different. One might argue that it is the patient's right to choose to do this, but therapeutic community staff would argue that this represents an unrealistic view of the patient's capacity to choose between alternatives.

> By suggesting to a client that they make their room their own we are providing clients with a space to take responsibility by making their own free choice about their room which will reflect their internal sense of self. If however the client responds by leaving their room exactly how it is, with clothes strewn about and without any personal objects in it and when we confront them about this the client says, 'This is how I want my room', we will not be educating the client to make their own free choices or nurturing their creative potential by leaving the client completely free from direction. If we leave the client at this point we will be leaving them stuck with their difficulty. (Tucker 1998)

However, if staff take too much control things just revert to the old custodial model, or turn into a staff-led skills training programme with no room for self-awareness and self-direction. What is required is for staff to be able to take the lead when structure is needed, and let go of it when patients begin to show that they can do things on their own initiative. In managing this delicate balance, therapeutic community staff are helped if they can understand the patient's be-haviour, and their own responses to it, in psychodynamic terms (as described in Chapter 3), recognizing that underlying fears or wishes may not be not ex-pressed openly, nor even acknowledged by the patient, yet may have a marked impact on someone who appears outwardly to be 'simply' lethargic or unmoti-vated. Understanding can help staff to manage their own frustration better and not retreat into treating patients in either an impersonal or a condescending way.

A major factor in developing a therapeutic community for people with chronic mental illness is the creation of small living and working groups of no more than fifteen or twenty people, sometimes subdivided into smaller family-like sub-groups. The size of such groups harks back to the early days of moral treatment. In contrast to the trivial, repetitive tasks that were fre-quently used to occupy patients' time in traditional psychiatric hospitals, the work will have some real and visible value. It may include the chores of do-mestic living, work of a practical nature such as gardening, farm work, build-ing, carpentry, or involvement in schemes to provide a service to another organization such as catering or cleaning. Many of these ideas are shared with other rehabilitative programmes. What is distinctive in the therapeutic community approach is the recognition that *just* focusing on work behaviour misses out the importance of how the patient-community member feels and thinks, the world of inner experience, and how he/she feels towards and re-lates towards other members of the group. Focus on these aspects is ad-dressed in regular group meetings.

Community meetings of the whole patient and staff group will take place anything between daily and once or twice a week, focusing on issues arising in the day-to-day life of the community. These may include problems at work, incidents in the living area, grievances felt by one member towards an-other, queries about their medication, and so on. Such meetings can be seen to have an underlying educative purpose of helping patients learn how to talk about their feelings rather than act on them impulsively, how to listen to others' points of view, and how to discuss and negotiate with others over a difference or conflict rather than get stuck in an oppose-or-retreat position. Smaller group meetings may also take place linked to particular tasks or ac-tivities, where patients may assess each other's work and discuss their feel-ings about working together.

An arrangement which can have special value in this kind of therapeutic community is bringing together staff and patients with people from the out-side community, in particular relatives, local employers or representatives of different services available to the patients. These 'outsiders' may be invited to attend community meetings or come for special meetings. The goals can be

to ease the anxieties that the 'outsiders' may have about the way patients behave by letting them see for themselves; and to prepare patients for more involvement with the outside world by gradually bringing them into contact
with parts of it.

Last and in some ways most important are the meetings for staff members.
They are particularly important in settings where the staff may not all have
chosen to work in this way, for example where people are allocated to wards
or units in ways which take little account of the match between the unit and
the individual. In this situation staff members can find themselves suddenly
expected to work in a way of which they have no experience and to which
they may even be opposed. They may be used to working in a clear-cut professional hierarchy with little opportunity for free discussion between people at the top and bottom of the hierarchy. Even less will they expect patients
to take an active part in organizing their own rehabilitation. An important
part of the work in this type of therapeutic community can therefore be in
persuading all the staff to accept and use the approach. Only if the staff team
as a whole believes that patients are capable of independent, responsible behaviour, and that regular meetings with open discussion of ward issues are
useful, will the therapeutic community flourish. The staff meeting is vital for
influencing staff attitudes, for discussion of the problems and anxieties that
arise from day to day, and as an actual demonstration that open discussion of
different viewpoints is both possible and helpful.

In addition to their programme of work and group activities, most institutional therapeutic communities use the major tranquilizing drugs to control
the psychotic elements in patients' thinking, such as delusions, thought disorder, and extremes of mood. For some patients anti-psychotic medication
may be indispensable in enabling them to participate in the social activities
of a therapeutic community.

THE THERAPEUTIC COMMUNITY APPROACH IN
THE COMMUNITY

The signs from the mid 1990s are that therapeutic communities are beginning
to re-emerge as a relevant model of care in both in the health service and the
voluntary sector. The Dean of the Royal College of Psychiatrists has suggested
that some of the therapy within a Community Psychiatry Service is found
within a therapeutic community approach' (Cox 1998). The work of Hinshelwood (1996) and Wallenberg Pachaly (1997) points to the value for
community psychiatry of tackling splits between different elements of a group,
helping clients to contain their own anxiety by providing a containing network
of relationships, and providing practitioners with a reflective space to examine

in a non-judgmental way the relationships between the different agencies involved in patient care.

As mental hospitals have closed, the range of alternative accommodation has increased, from twenty-four-hour staffed hospital hostels with up to twenty beds through to ordinary houses and apartments for two or three or four people where someone calls in once a day to see how they are getting on together. Hostels and group homes are run by a number of statutory bodies in the fields of health, social service and criminal justice, and by many independent charitable organizations. The ways of running them take in the whole spectrum from highly authoritarian establishments to very permissive, egalitarian ones.

A common arrangement is for a housing association to form a partnership with a therapy organization and set up a hostel or group home for people with mental health problems. The best-known pioneer of this approach in the mental health field is probably the Richmond Fellowship which during the 1960s and 1970s established over thirty houses in Great Britain as well as several in the United States and Australia. The Fellowship was the creation of Elly Jansen, who as a Dutch theology student in London set up a hostel in 1959 for ex-psychiatric patients. Its success led to the setting up of a second hostel with staff and residents from the first. As it grew the Fellowship developed a standard structure which included residents organizing and doing the household chores from 9–11 a.m. every morning (apart from those who had moved on to take outside jobs), obligatory attendance of all residents and staff at a weekly community meeting, weekly individual and group therapy sessions for each resident, and participation in various work projects (Jansen 1980). Members of staff performed both administrative and therapeutic tasks in order to avoid a split between these two aspects of staff–resident relationships. The size of the staff team in each house was small by hospital standards – typically four or five for twelve to twenty residents. As a national organization the Richmond Fellowship was able to support newly established houses and to provide its own career structure, with a two-year in-service staff training programme. Unfortunately in the late 1980s the organization found itself in difficulties with the Charity Commission and was broken up into different organizations. A number of staff went off to develop new therapeutic community projects, such as Community Housing and Therapy and Threshold.

Today Community Housing and Therapy (CHT) runs five residential projects for between nine and fifteen severely mentally ill people in and around London. It uses a particular therapeutic community approach which is grounded in an educative framework aimed at enabling clients to become active citizens (Tucker 1998). Threshold operates in Northern Ireland where it has four residential therapeutic communities for adults plus supported flats, a training and research unit, and also offers therapeutic intervention services to children and adolescents (Moore 1998).

An earlier pioneering venture of this kind was St Luke's Project which was started in Chelsea, London in 1974 'to break the cycle of re-admission'. The project developed a number of day centres in the same neighbourhood, each with its own therapeutic model designed for clients with different needs and capabilities. A primary attachment model was used for apathetic, unmotivated clients, often with chronic mental illness; a re-socializing model was used for people with chronic psychosis who, with the help of medication, were able to participate in a communal environment; a re-educative model was used with people with borderline personality disorders and chronic neurosis who were capable of benefiting from group therapy; finally a re-constructive model was developed for people with similar diagnoses to the previous group but with greater psychological mindedness and motivation to change (Blake *et al.* 1984).

THERAPEUTIC COMMUNITIES FOR ACUTE PSYCHIATRIC DISORDERS

The 1990s has seen the demise of well-staffed high-morale psychiatric admission wards within larger psychiatric hospitals. Such wards would often have contained a mixture of acutely disturbed individuals and more long-term mentally ill people who were re-admitted for a few weeks or months from time to time. The present philosophy is to treat acute mental illness in the community where possible, and to manage those with long-term illness in hostels and day centres. This has had two effects. One is that only the most disturbed and difficult-to-treat people are admitted to acute admission wards. The other is that such wards are now somewhat isolated, often in a general hospital environment, and lack the morale and expertise they once contained. The result has been an unhappy regression to a version of psychiatric in-patient care that places the emphasis on control. Yet for quite a long period the therapeutic community approach was associated with some exemplary models of acute in-patient psychiatry.

Therapeutic communities of the democratic analytic type were not originally intended for acutely disturbed psychotic patients, but between the 1950s and 1980s a small number of psychiatrists in Britain, Europe and America were sufficiently influenced by therapeutic community ideas, and in particular by Maxwell Jones' work, to attempt to run their acute wards on therapeutic community lines (Wilmer 1958, Mandelbrote 1965, Clark 1966, Almond 1974). How they actually did this varied considerably, from simply holding a daily community meeting to creating a highly organized environment with an elaborate system of patient roles and group activities. In most cases these units continued to use drugs and ECT to treat the bio-chemical aspect of the patient's disturbance, but physical restraint and seclu-sion were used much less, if at all. Being able to talk about outbursts of aggressive behaviour in ward meetings enabled many crises to be contained. Generally the staff retained responsibility for decisions affecting treatment, although problems and requests concerning medication or discharge could be discussed openly between patients and staff. The staff also had to be ac-tive in creating and maintaining the community norms since patients stayed a relatively short time – often only a matter of weeks.

The goals of treatment in these units were in part the same as those in any admission unit – to reduce patients' level of overt disturbance so that they could return home as soon as possible. Added to this was sometimes the goal that patients would learn to behave in an acceptable way and would not make use of their illness as an excuse for any antisocial behaviour which actually was within their control. This goal required delicate judgment since too strident an insistence on normal behaviour could overlook the reality, to the patient, of his or her difficulties; yet undoubtedly the expectations of those around the patient could influence his or her behaviour.

Another aspect of a therapeutic community admission ward was that it could enhance the overall running of the unit. Daily meetings would ensure that all patients were regularly seen and thought about, while the relative ab-sence of formality and hierarchy helped to create good staff relationships and ensure that support was readily available at times of crisis. The mainte-nance of good group morale could also enhance the effect of more specific treatments. All this is not to minimize the particular difficulties of this appli-cation of therapeutic community ideas. The fast rate of turnover among pa-tients and the highly disturbed state of some patients on admission could mean frequent disruptions to the daily programme and rapid changes in the level of responsibility patients were able to take. One week patients could be organizing an outing, the next they could be angrily demanding that the staff take charge of everything. Such work was seldom dull and often frus-trating.

One way to cope with these fluctuations is to have highly structured roles and expectations to which the new patient is introduced – emphasizing from the start the expectations of 'normal' behaviour. (The feasibility of this ap-proach may depend on whether there is somewhere else to send patients who are too disruptive to fit into it.) An example of this type of unit in America was Tomkins I which was opened in 1960 in the Yale-New Haven Community Hospital and has been extensively studied and written about. A number of specific roles were introduced for patients to help them take re-

which decided which patients were ready for passes to leave the ward, a 'buddy system' which enabled new patients to go off the ward if accompanied by another who had a pass, and Psychiatric Trustees who took responsibility for more disturbed patients. Suggestions for some of these roles came initially from the patients and were then incorporated into the unit's routine (Almond 1974).

In England two well-known units were Street Ward at Fulbourn Hospital in Cambridge and the Phoenix Unit at Littlemore Hospital in Oxford. At Street Ward new patients were met by the duty nurse and by the 'duty resident', a patient elected for the week, who gave them a tour of the unit. A booklet explained how the community worked and gave practical information such as maps and bus timetables. In addition to the community meetings, specific meetings were held to cater for different needs, including group therapy, the day-to-day affairs of washing-up rotas, etc., and patients' requests regarding their treatment (Pullen 1982). The Phoenix Unit was run in a less elaborately structured way, with less emphasis on formal roles and group tasks, and more on the general quality of support for patients and staff (Mandelbrote 1965, Sugarman 1968). Daily community meetings and small groups provided a framework within which staff encouraged patients to participate at whatever level they were able. Expectations of what role patients took were not predetermined and depended on individuals' capabilities and motivation. Activities such as cooking, art and psychodrama were optional. A consistent emphasis was on the staff meetings, in particular the weekly unstructured meeting of the whole staff, which numbered around thirty (including students from several disciplines). Here problems of integrating new staff, supporting those who felt under pressure, sharing anxieties about particular patients, and keeping everyone aware of the tensions inevitable in large groups were among the issues which regularly came up for discussion.

In Finland a therapeutic community for acute psychiatric patients was run for twenty years on a closed ward at the Department of Psychiatry of the University of Oulu. Between the early 1970s and the closure of the ward in 1993 over 1500 patients were treated in a weekly programme which included community groups, small groups, physical exercise, treatment planning sessions, departure groups, and (this being Finland) a sauna session on Friday evenings! Some sixty papers were published by Matti Isohanni and his colleagues, making this probably the most intensively evaluated of all acute psychiatric services run as therapeutic communities (Isohanni 1993).

Patients in admission units are necessarily unselected for any particular form of treatment, so that the programme of treatment, whether therapeutic community or not, must be flexible enough to incorporate people with very different problems and needs. Units specifically for young schizophrenics have also been run as therapeutic communities. At Chestnut Lodge in Maryland, America, a small therapeutic community was created in which ample nursing and medical staff made it possible to deal with even severe management problems by psychosocial means rather than medication (McGlashen and Levy 1977). Two other units for young schizophrenics, Soteria in the United States and Villa 21 in England, are described in Chapter 8.

A number of therapeutic communities for psychotic patients have been established in Italy over the last twenty years following the law passed in 1978 banning further admissions to psychiatric hospital. These are part of what are called 'intermediate structures' which have been created to fill the gap between general hospital wards and out-patient facilities. They draw on a range of theoretical frameworks including psychoanalysis, therapeutic communities, cognitive behaviour therapy and dialectical behaviour therapy (Caltagirone and Smargiassi 1997).

Perhaps most radical has been the development of a therapeutic community that meets for just one day a fortnight (Markezinis et al. 1992). This is one of the innovations pioneered at the Open Psychotherapeutic Centre since its foundation in Athens in 1980 (Tsegos 1982). People are able to attend while maintaining a job or who live a long way from the Centre. A sense of community is created through participation in different formal and informal activities together, and staff at the Centre report that this format is capable of sustaining quite disturbed patients at home. The model of an intensive therapeutic community meeting for one day a fortnight has many interesting implications in terms of cost, maintaining people in their own homes and jobs, and offering services to a wide geographical area.

CHAPTER 7

Concept-based Therapeutic Communities for Drug Abusers

THE STORY OF SYNANON

The therapeutic communities described in the previous chapters have one important thing in common. They were created by people like doctors, teachers and social workers working in places like hospitals, schools, hostels, prisons, and so on. In other words, by qualified staff working within the established framework of care-giving professions and institutions. In 1958 a quite new kind of therapeutic community was created by a group of ex-alcoholics and drug addicts. It was called Synanon, and it was the first of what have come to be known as concept-based therapeutic communities. This name refers to their adherence to a set of explicit concepts about the nature of drug addiction and its treatment. Communities of this type have since been established in Europe, South Africa, Australia and the Far East as well as throughout their native United States.

The inspiration behind Synanon and its successors was provided by an ex-alcoholic called Chuck Dederich. A former oil company executive, in 1958 Dederich was unemployed and living in Ocean Park, a 'slum' district in California. He began holding a weekly discussion group in his apartment, inviting friends from Alcoholics Anonymous (AA), of which he was at that time still a member, to participate. Dederich described these as 'free-association' meetings with no particular agenda, although many of the participants had a psychoanalytic orientation. The sociologist Lewis Yablonsky quotes him as saying:

> The meetings were loud and boisterous. Attack of one another was a keynote of the sessions, with everyone joining in. I could detect considerable lying and self-deception in the group. I began to attack viciously partly out of my own irritations and at times to defend myself. The group would join in, and we would let the air out of pompously inflated egos, including my own. The sessions soon became the high point in everybody's week. (Yablonsky 1965)

The meetings increased to three nights a week, and more people began attending – at this stage still mostly ex-alcoholics. The members decided to rent a building as a 'clubhouse' where they could meet during the day. Already it was becoming apparent that some were being helped to reduce their intake of alcohol or drugs. Soon members began bringing their friends, who included one or two long-term drug addicts trying to 'kick' the habit. Dederich told one of them, an incorrigible addict called Jesse, that if he wanted to succeed he would have to move in and live there. Jesse stayed, and stayed off drugs. It was then, Dederich later said, that he realized he had a new career.

At this stage, Synanon included both ex-addicts and alcoholics. The two groups did not get on well together and a rift soon occurred with the local branch of AA. From that time on, Synanon was concerned primarily with the rehabilitation of former drug addicts. The way Synanon got its name provides an interesting reflection of its aim to help its members improve their general education. In addition to the 'attack' groups, Dederich had initiated educational seminars with readings from the works of Freud and religious and philosophical writers. A newly arrived ex-addict, unfamiliar with words like symposium and seminar, had stammered out the request to go to 'another of those sym … sem … synanons'.

Having realized that he had a career, Dederich got things organized. Using his knowledge of business, he registered the club as a non-profit making organization, called The Synanon Foundation. He also began to formulate his ideas about the way it worked, and when a group of parole officers who were impressed by Synanon's early success invited Dederich to give a talk, he gave a speech that included the following statement:

> We have here a climate consisting of a family structure similar in some areas to a primitive tribal structure, which … also contains overtones of a nineteenth-century family of the type which produced inner-directed personalities. A more or less autocratic family structure appears to be necessary to buy some time for the recovering addict. This time is then used to administer doses of an inner-directed philosophy such as that outlined in Emerson's essay entitled Self Reliance. If it seems paradoxical that an authoritative environment tends to produce inner direction, it must be remembered that the inner directed men of the nineteenth century were products of an authoritative family structure. (Yablonsky 1965)[1]

---

1 The term 'inner directed' was coined by the sociologist David Riesman (1969), who described three types of personality associated with three types of society: tradition directed, inner directed and other directed. Inner-directed people are influenced not by what other people say or do but by their own inner values and convictions.

We can see here the importance, early in the development of concept-based communities, of the model of an autocratic family with (not stated but implied) the director as its head. The assumption that this would create inner-directed personalities was probably incorrect, for Synanon also created an openness and intimacy which would not have been found in the kind of families Dederich was thinking of. Nevertheless it indicates the importance attached to philosophical and moral values – which later became the 'concepts'.

It is interesting that Dederich refers to 'doses' of philosophy as if it were medicine. Although in fact offering a powerful alternative to medical treatment, it is possible that in addressing a professional audience he wanted to use an image that would be readily understood and that would help Synanon to be accepted as a legitimate alternative to medical treatment. It is interesting how such a scenario resembles William Tuke's efforts to appeal to the medical profession of his time. Later on relations with the outside world, and professionals in particular, were to become less friendly for Synanon.

A daily routine took shape at Synanon that was to form the model for all future concept-based communities. It included daily job assignments, regular 'synanons' (the term referred to the attack therapy groups as well as the organization as a whole), and daily discussions around philosophical readings. During 1959 there was a shift from residents still using small amounts of drugs to those staying completely 'clean' – i.e. drug free – and already the importance of 'role models' was emerging. These were former addicts who had succeeded in giving up drugs, to whom new arrivals could look as examples to follow. This fitted in with the idea of a family in which these 'models' were like older brothers or sisters.

A year and a half after its first beginnings, Synanon, now with fifty residents, moved to new premises in Santa Monica, a well-to-do Los Angeles suburb. The arrival of this mixed group of blacks and whites, many with criminal records, in a smart white residential area was greeted with predictable hostility by the local inhabitants. They tried to get Synanon moved, on the grounds that it was really a hospital and was infringing certain 'zoning' regulations. Official reports and court hearings followed and at one stage Dederich was actually imprisoned for a brief period for infringing zoning regulations. Eventually State and Federal committees were called on to assess Synanon. They made reports in its favour, seeing it as 'a most promising effort to rehabilitate narcotic addicts'. After a three-year public battle Synanon was officially approved, and it developed rapidly into a large organization, spawning several new communities and inspiring many copies.

In California and Nevada (a neighbouring state) new communities were set up. Ex-addicts were invited to run Synanon groups for addicts in prison, sometimes where they themselves had been former inmates. However, the largest problem of addiction in America was in New York, and it was there that the major derivatives of Synanon developed. The first, Daytop Village, was started in 1963 by a team of psychiatrists and probation officers who had been impressed by a visit to Synanon. In its first year the project did not go well, and the organizers appointed a graduate of Synanon to take over as director. He immediately changed Daytop from a loosely regulated 'half-way house' tolerating illicit drug use, to a tightly run therapeutic community with the same rules and values as Synanon. After three years as a successful Synanon-style community a major conflict developed between the ex-addict director and the board of management, which included psychiatrists and priests, over who was in control. The director left, taking many of the staff and residents with him. Dan Casriel, a psychiatrist who had been a member of the team which established Daytop, took over as director and the community re-established itself (Sugarman 1974). The potential for conflict between professional and ex-addict staff is discussed later in this chapter. In 1968 another major organization was launched: Phoenix House, New York. Started with the help of Daytop and initially staffed by former Synanon residents, it became the largest and best-known concept house, with places for about four hundred residents at any one time.

The Concept-based Therapeutic Community Goes Global

In 1970 three graduates from Phoenix House came to Britain to start a community in London, and in subsequent years concept-based communities were set up in Oxford, Portsmouth, Sheffield and Dublin. During this period communities were also established in many European countries, notably Holland, Sweden and West Germany. Since then the spread of therapeutic communities for ex-drug addicts has become worldwide, extending to six continents and nearly sixty countries.

The American-based International Council on Alcoholism and Addiction formed a therapeutic communities section which since 1976 has organized an annual World Conference of Therapeutic Communities – a slightly misleading title in that its main concern is with drug addiction rather than the whole range of problems treated in different types of therapeutic communities. In 1980 this development led to the formation of the World Federation of Therapeutic Communities, followed by separate Federations in Europe, Asia and Latin America, devoted to working with and influencing governments in planning how the problems of addiction should be tackled at a national and international level. Back in the United States two national projects were launched in late 1980s and early 1990s in response to the growing number being sent to prison for drug offences. This resulted in an increase from 25 prison-based therapeutic communities in 1987 to 110 in 1997, making concept-based therapeutic communities the 'treatment of choice' in American prisons (Lipton 1997, Wexler 1997).

The End of Synanon

Synanon changed its character during the 1970s from a therapeutic community, with the goal of returning ex-addicts to society as productive citizens, to a permanent alternative way of life. Synanon City, as it called itself, attracted a large number of 'straights' (non-addicts) as well as former addicts, who came to live there because they preferred its values and lifestyle to those of society at large. As Synanon became more inward looking, Dederich increasingly became a dictator whom no one could challenge. In 1975 Synanon proclaimed itself a religion, with an aggressive policy towards any opposition. Things came to a head in 1978 when Dederich and others were arrested on a charge of conspiracy. They had attempted to kill a lawyer involved in a legal action brought against Synanon by some relatives of people who had gone to live there. It was the disastrous collapse of a career which had spanned twenty years and given rise to a flourishing worldwide network of therapeutic communities.

The story of Synanon is difficult to be impartial about. From one point of view – that of its creators and supporters – it was a uniquely successful attempt to create an effective form of self-help for otherwise hopeless drug addicts. From another point of view – that of some professionals and some relatives of those attracted to Synanon – it was a cult which brainwashed its members into total acceptance of its values and lifestyle. The truth is difficult to disentangle; both views contain some of it. Any powerful belief system can be both salvation and entrapment. Which view you take depends partly on whether you agree with the particular beliefs and also on how those who lead such a movement use or misuse their power. We will return to consider some of these issues later in the chapter.

HOW CONCEPT-BASED THERAPEUTIC COMMUNITIES WORK

An informed opinion about concept-based therapeutic communities requires an understanding of what they are trying to do: how they view the problem of drug addiction and how they set about tackling it. We will consider this under two headings, the structure of activities and the concepts.

THE STRUCTURE OF ACTIVITIES

The style of operation evolved at Synanon in its first few years set the pattern for all its successors. Today staff from concept-based communities around the world can meet and discuss their work with some certainty that their communities resemble each other in their overall structure and the terms they use. The main features include total drug abstinence, a hierarchical work structure, confrontational group sessions modelled on the Synanon, and a range of educational and social activities. In addition to these basic elements there is an overall atmosphere or culture of close mutual surveillance and intense pressure on everyone to be actively engaged with and concerned for others. Some communities have also incorporated a variety of group techniques from the humanistic and behavioural models.

Drug abstinence

Because the communities are primarily for ex-drug addicts who want to learn to live without drugs, abstinence from all mind-affecting drugs – including alcohol – is a cardinal rule. The possibility of social drinking is not entertained during the residents' treatment. Communities differ as to whether they condone it in the later phases of rehabilitation. The attitude to the use of illegal drugs, including cannabis, is clear-cut – any use is unacceptable by staff or residents. This attitude derives from the view that it is the drug-taking subculture, not the drug itself, which is the chief enemy, and that drug use inevitably involves contact with this subculture. In order to emphasize this rule, and make it easier to enforce, no drugs or alcohol are allowed on the premises. Prospective residents are interviewed away from the community and new residents are searched on arrival. Some communities extend the ban on addictive substances to cigarettes.

Hierarchical work structure

Residents are responsible for the entire day-to-day servicing of the community, to an exacting level of precision and tidiness. Communities are often situated in large houses which have seen better days and offer considerable scope for maintenance work. The work is carried out and supervised through a hierarchy of residents, carefully structured so that each position has defined duties and each level carries wider responsibilities than the one below it. In contrast to the democratic analytic communities the structure is designed to heighten the differences between each level of responsibility. The hierarchy applies only during work, not to relationships outside work time.

The following, based on the Ley Community in Oxford, is probably fairly typical for a community of twenty to thirty residents. This hierarchy has a number of functions. The precise expectations of task performance are in marked contrast to the lifestyle of most drug addicts. The structure provides an antidote for people whose lives have been very disorganized before joining the community. The hierarchy is also an achievable status system. Whereas in society most drug addicts fail to achieve any position of success, in the therapeutic community they can climb from being a crew member en-

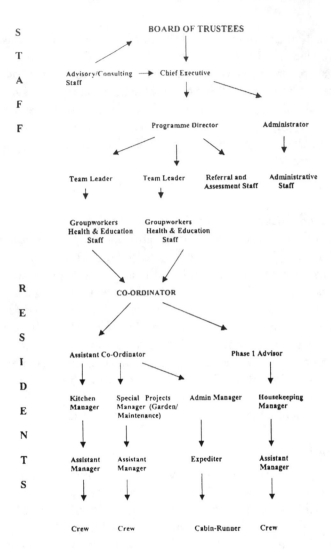

Figure 7.1 Example of heirarchy in a concept-based therapeutic community

gaged in menial jobs to becoming the co-ordinator with responsibility and prestige. A resident can eventually become a staff member and director of a community. The hierarchy also symbolizes the family of which Dederich spoke. Those at the bottom are the 'babies' with no responsibilities for others. Those halfway up are like older brothers and sisters, with responsibility for their younger 'siblings', while those at the top are the adults or parents of the family. Lastly, the hierarchy is a very practical preparation for work in the outside world, of which few addicts will have had much experience.

Each department is fully responsible for one aspect of the day-to-day running of the community. On arrival new residents are put into one of the work crews where they are expected to carry out instructions willingly and respectfully, and to be aware of what they are doing. Many addicts take little notice of their surroundings, and new residents are often told to go over the job they have just done in order to make them attend to every detail. Crew members are also expected to converse while working, not to use work as an escape from relationships. The supervisor (assistant manager) notices and 'passes up' information on the crew members' work performance and on their attitudes and social behaviour. The manager is responsible for organizing the work, deciding what, how and when tasks should be tackled, and for passing up information to the co-ordinator. Such responsibility can be quite stressful. A manager who makes a mess of things may be 'shot down' – i.e. demoted back to the level of crew member so as to relearn the simpler levels of responsibility, and have time to sort themselves out before having another go at a responsible position.

The co-ordinator and assistant co-ordinator are responsible for keeping in touch not only with the progress of the different departments but with the attitudes and behaviour of all the residents. If someone is being slack, rude, or otherwise not conforming they may be called into the co-ordinator's office for a 'talking to' or a 'haircut' – a verbal dressing down. The co-ordinator informs the staff of any problems and asks their advice about dealing with difficulties. The staff go through the co-ordinator and managers in organizing activities and implementing decisions. It is important for maintaining the hierarchy that the staff are seen to go through the 'proper channels' rather than approach crew members directly.

One consequence of the hierarchy is that a relatively small number of staff can manage the community, for their job is less to provide the therapeutic relationships themselves than to maintain the community's culture at its optimum. At best the community functions rather like a well-tuned engine, but there are a number of ways in which it can start to falter. Too much pressure to conform may cause residents to leave, or find covert ways of opting out. Too little pressure may lead to a loss of group cohesion and commitment. Residents will be quick to spot loopholes in a system and exploit them. The effectiveness of this kind of community requires that there be few loopholes or escape routes (other than leaving). Constant surveillance by the staff and swift response to deviant behaviour are needed to keep the 'engine' running well. It also provides an important demonstration of the staff's sincerity and interest. Even negative attention may be valued. One resident was worried that he had not had a 'talking to' for two months, as he thought this meant the others were not really interested in him.

Encounter groups

These are the type of verbally aggressive 'no holds-barred' group developed at Synanon. They provide an essential balance to the structured working relationships. The work hierarchy creates pressures which bring to the surface feelings and attitudes which can be expressed and then examined in the encounter groups.

The groups may be held two or three times a week, lasting for two to three hours, sometimes longer. There may be simultaneous groups each with ten or twelve residents. Membership of each of these groups is not constant but is decided on the basis of which residents need to be in the same group to deal with their current relationships. This practice is in contrast to the democratic analytic communities in which regular group membership is considered necessary, which leads members to develop a strong attachment to 'their' small group. In a concept-based community the main attachment is to the community as a whole.

The encounter group follows an established procedure. In the first phase several members confront a particular individual over some aspect of his or her recent behaviour or attitude. The indictments are made at ear-splitting volume. For example, the crew members of one of the work departments may shout and curse at their supervisor (violence and threats are forbidden) whose instructions were confusing or inconsistent. The supervisor may in turn scream back at them for being lazy or sloppy, or may decide to sit there and brave it out. This phase is intended to break through the individual's defensive barrier, while also allowing tensions to be discharged. There follows a phase of frank, probing discussion of the difficulties which the resident is having in the community at that time. For example, a male resident in the position of supervisor may be feeling lonely and isolated, afraid that if he behaves in an authoritative way others won't like him. Following this phase of the encounter several others may share their own similar feelings, and the resident is finally given some advice about how to cope with immediate difficulties. This often includes a reaffirmation of the commitment to stay in the community and get more involved with the other members. The group then passes on to focus on another member and the shouting begins again.

These groups can appear daunting to the newcomer – a new resident may take some weeks before learning to bellow out feelings with full force. They may seem to be a vehicle for scapegoating, but emphasis is placed on the need for confrontation to come from concern for the other person rather than rejection. In fact the encounter groups can generate considerable warmth and closeness between its members. In a sense they are an initiation ceremony into intimacy. Once residents have been through the hail of verbal attacks they may start to feel much closer to one another than they could otherwise have done.

Social confidence training

Another range of activities is intended to give residents the general knowledge, skills and confidence which they have previously lacked to deal with social situations. There are frequent seminars when one resident gives a talk to the others on a subject which the resident has prepared in advance. These will include presentation of the concepts to new residents. There are impromptu speaking sessions when residents take it in turns to stand up and speak on a topic without any preparation. The more experienced residents go out on speaking engagements, when they describe the work of the community and their own life histories to audiences from interested organizations. And there are the daily morning meetings. These are not unstructured community meetings but a cross between school assembly and party games. Announcements are made, backsliders are spotlighted, belief in the value of the community is reaffirmed, and then some members will be expected to drop their 'image' and entertain the others with a funny song or act. I can say from experience that this is good for inhibited professionals as well as ex-addicts.

Relating

In addition to coping with these more formal social situations, residents are expected to spend much of their free time 'relating' to each other in pairs, talking about their feelings and getting to know the other person. Spare time – after meals or in the morning – is not to be spent alone. Opportunities for relating to outsiders occur on 'open house' days when relatives and local people are invited in. Such events occasion a good deal of nervousness among the residents who, having grown to feel at ease with each other, need to test out their social skills with other people.

Phases of treatment

Most concept-based communities divide up treatment into three main phases. The description given so far applies to the second phase when the resident is living, working and relating to others exclusively in the community, progressing up the resident hierarchy. This may last around twelve months. Preceding this is an induction/orientation phase of around one to two months, and following it is the re-entry phase which can last between six and twelve months. During re-entry the resident looks for a job outside and begins to go out in the evening while still living in the community. In the last phase, he leaves, often getting a flat or house with residents who are leaving at the same time. In America therapeutic communities in prisons have developed aftercare programmes to provide ex-addicts vocational training and drug-free housing once they leave prison. At a later date if they have stayed 'clean' and kept within the law they will become 'graduates' of the community. Some communities mark graduation with a special dinner and a graduation ring, modelling themselves on the American college.

THE CONCEPTS

The rationale for this approach has been expressed in a number of simple, clear explanations of the psychological causes of drug addiction and how the therapeutic community will enable life to be lived without drugs. These explanations are known as 'the concepts'. They picture drug addicts as people with a particular kind of personality: anxious and self-doubting, needing to convince themselves and others of a success that isn't real and so unable to risk close, honest relationships, leading impulsive self-centred lives oblivious of the people around them except when they can be used to meet the addict's own needs. The concepts minimize the importance of family, social and economic factors. These may have contributed to the addict's plight, but it is he or she who is seen as responsible for the response to these conditions. No one has to be a drug addict, so it is up to the individual to choose, and to change.

The availability of simple, direct concepts, rather than the more complex theories which professionals tend to use (such as psychoanalysis) helps residents to experience a sense of mastery over their previously helpless situation. This finding has been increasingly recognized by professional therapists in recent years, with 'user-friendly' models such as transactional analysis and cognitive behaviour therapy. Maxwell Jones also recognized this in his early days at Mill Hill, where he explained in lectures to his effort syndrome patients the physiology of their symptoms. Being able to understand and explain to others how one's difficulties were caused is of considerable value in motivating someone for the effort that personal change involves. Indeed it is probably one of the key elements in all self-help movements and in many religious movements too.

The concepts can be grouped into three sorts: those which explain the nature of the addict's problems, those which demonstrate how therapy works, and those which underline how he ought (and ought not) to conduct himself in the community. You may wonder how the same explanations can apply equally to everyone. The answer seems to be that they are sufficiently general, and that drug addicts have sufficient experiences in common, for this to be effective. The latter point is important – addicts share many common experiences and psychological characteristics. The concepts would not necessarily apply to a wider cross-section of psychologically disturbed people.

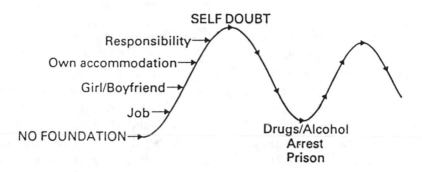

Figure 7.2 The roller coaster

The following examples come from the early years of Phoenix House, New York.

The roller coaster

This concept explains to the new resident the pattern of his life prior to joining the community, and makes sense of his failure to achieve success and stability up till now. It shows how temporary enthusiasm leads to short-lived achievements, but without a foundation of self-knowledge the responsibilities cannot be borne. Anxiety and self-doubt lead to things going wrong and before he knows

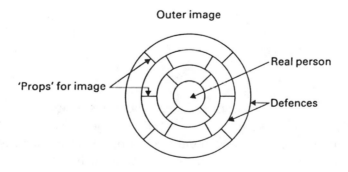

Figure 7.3 The onion

it he is back on drugs and in trouble with the law. The cycle repeats itself, getting worse each time.

The onion

This concept illustrates the kind of defence many addicts use to distance themselves from other people. Addicts are often 'image-conscious' young people – for example appearing to be tough, aloof, cool, relaxed. The onion concept explains that such appearances are a protection against letting others see them, or even against seeing themselves, as they really are. The 'props' for an image might include styles of dress, hair, 'street talk', and so on. In the therapeutic community these props are taken away; residents are required, for example, to dress in a fairly conventional way so that these image defences can be broken through and the real person revealed.

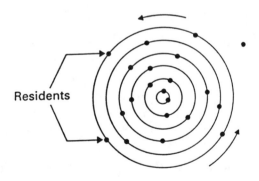

Figure 7.4 The community wheel

The community wheel

This explains life in the therapeutic community, which is compared to a spinning wheel. New residents are on the outside at first and are at risk of 'flying off'. They have to work their way into the centre by involving themselves in everything that goes on. Those near the centre are more stable and less likely to fly off. There is a picture of the community wheel on a wall with every resident's name on it. Residents can move each other's names to where they feel that person is at the time.

Act as if

This is one of the most important concepts concerning how residents should behave in the community. It is explained that much of the addict's problems come from acting impulsively. In the community they are expected to learn self-control. While working in their department they should not let irritation or frustration show and should act in a calm, tolerant, cordial manner. If they feel apathetic or negative they should act motivated. The place to deal with the feelings is in the encounter groups. Such an injunction is intended to provide an antidote to the addict's previous failure to cope with feelings and impulses, by teaching residents how to function despite them.

More than other types of therapeutic community, the concept-based communities are explicitly and unashamedly value based. George De Leon, who has been one of the key figures researching and writing in this field over the past twenty years, has put forward his ideas for a general theoretical model. Central to this is a view of 'right living'.

The view of right living emphasizes explicit values that guide how individuals relate to themselves, peers, significant others and the larger society. These include truth and honesty (in word and deed), the work ethic, learning to learn, personal accountability, economic self-reliance, responsible concern for peers, family responsibility, community involvement and good citizenry.

The ideological and psychological views of the therapeutic community perspective are integrated into its teachings and methods to achieve [these] specific social and psychological goals. (De Leon 1994 p.20)

The growth of concept-based therapeutic communities around the world attests to their effectiveness in treating drug addiction, at least for those addicts with the commitment and capacity to stay in treatment for some months. However, the model has also been controversial, containing within it elements that have a destructive potential if not carefully managed. While this is true of any powerful therapeutic medium, including other types of therapeutic community, the concept-based model poses some particular questions.

THREE ISSUES

Concept-based therapeutic communities have attracted controversy for three reasons. First, the requirement of conformity. They have what amounts to a complete handbook of behaviour, attitudes and values, which applies to everything that goes on from getting up in the morning to relaxing in the evening, and they use a wide array of methods for inducing conformity and commitment to these rules and values, some of which have earned criticism. Second, the position of ex-addict staff in relation to staff with professional backgrounds. This relationship is ambiguous – equal in some ways, not in others – and has at times become fraught. Third, the risk of therapeutic zeal sliding unchecked into a Messianic conviction of rightness. Synanon's antecedents and eventual end has raised the question of whether this type of therapeutic community is a cultural breakthrough, as has been argued, or a dangerous cult. Let us look at these issues in turn.

PRESSURE TO CONFORM

Much of the foregoing description has implied the use of rewards and punishments, although these terms are seldom used within a community. The communities themselves see a 'haircut' (verbal dressing down) or 'shooting someone down' the hierarchy not as punishment but as giving the individual greater self-awareness. Promotion to a new position is seen less as a reward than as an opportunity to 'stretch out' and acquire greater skills and self-confidence. From this point of view what matters is that such events have an understandable meaning for the resident, and do not repeat his experience of a hostile world simply handing out punishment to a resentful offender.

This needs to be emphasized because concept-based communities have aroused the disquiet of professionals for some of their methods for dealing with serious transgressions of the community's norms, such as stealing or using drugs. These methods have included shaving a man's head (women wear stocking caps), or hanging a placard around someone's neck with words on it which describe the problem in stark terms, for example 'I steal things because I can't ask for love. Please help me.' The purpose of such measures is to shock the individual into awareness of the seriousness of his problem – the same aim as the 'reality confrontation' described by Rapaport (1960) in therapeutic communities run on democratic lines. However, they can also seem to the outsider as degrading and humiliating, and relatives of residents and well-meaning professionals have sometimes been indignant at their use. As a result many communities have given them up in favour of less controversial devices. The important point, however, is how they are seen by the persons involved. In a community where there is an atmosphere of concern, to which the individual is responsive, they may be felt as acceptable forms of penance, to change attitudes and behaviour. In the absence of such an atmosphere, they may only be humiliating and the outsider's viewpoint might be nearer the mark.

In addition to these dramatic acts there is a wide range of more conventional privileges and sanctions which are in effect a system of rewards and punishments. Such a system would be called a behaviour modification programme if provided by professional staff in a conventional psychiatric setting. Permission to write and receive letters, to go out alone, or spend time on favourite interests, are all privileges controlled by the staff. By withdrawing all such rights at first, the new resident is pushed into total involvement with the community. (The pioneers of moral treatment in the nineteenth century had the same idea, and forbade new patients contact with the outside world, especially with close relatives as they were considered to be part of the problem.) Once the resident has established a secure bond with the community (the 'baby' stage has been passed) he is given his 'privileges' and can begin to move out into the wider world.

Despite these and other devices for inducing conformity and commitment, it is likely that none of them is actually as potent an influence on behaviour as the relationships between residents. While residents in their first few months may go through the motions of showing concern for others, eventually this becomes quite genuine. Being physically held and accepted by another resident while the most painful and frightening feelings are being experienced creates feelings of great closeness and trust. After six months residents may feel closer to their peers than they have ever felt to anyone in their lives. Such mutual concern or love is a far more powerful influence on behaviour than the formal system of sanctions. The confrontation of a resident for a 'bad attitude' comes then, not from dutiful conformity, but from a concern that both the confronter and the confronted should 'make it through the programme' together.

EX-ADDICTS AND PROFESSIONALS WORKING TOGETHER AS STAFF MEMBERS

Ex-addicts who have successfully completed their own rehabilitation can work as staff members in concept-based communities. Indeed it is the presence among the staff of role models who were once addicts themselves and are now in positions of responsibility and authority that gives these therapeutic communities their unique credibility in the field of addiction treatment. There is also some evidence that graduates of programmes with ex-addict staff are less likely to relapse than graduates of programmes run exclusively by professionals (Lipton 1997). In practice, however, ex-addict staff will usually be working alongside professionally qualified staff because it is the latter who are in a position to organize treatment projects, to get funds and to hire staff. Synanon was created by ex-addicts on their own, but few communities have the organizing genius of a Dederich.

There are also some arguable advantages in having a mixed staff team in which ex-addicts and professional staff balance each other's contribution and points of view. The ex-addicts' personal experience of the damaging, potentially lethal, effects of drug addiction makes them strongly committed to helping others learn to live without drugs. It also makes them quick to recognize the persuasive deceits and rationalizations that addicts use with professional helpers. Having been through such a community themselves they can empathize with what residents are feeling, and (most important from the resident's point of view) the ex-addict staff member offers a living example of someone like themselves who has succeeded in making a life without drugs.

Professional staff can contribute the 'outsider' perspective of alternative views and experience, while the simple fact of their presence and involvement offers a useful antidote to ex-addict staff as well as residents. For residents they may provide the first experience of concerned and empathic authority figures. For ex-addict staff who still have a stereotyped picture of 'straight' people as dull and conventional but also as emotionally untroubled, close working contact can break down this stereotype and show that 'straights' have problems too. Professionals can contribute to the ideas which the staff use in their work, and can help to create a forum for examining authority issues. A regular sensitivity or 'staff maintenance' meeting of ex-addict and professional staff will enable the staff to discuss problems in a more open and non-judgmental way.

There is a risk in such a mixed staff team that the basic principles of the community will be eroded, and it is important that the concepts and hierarchical structure are not undermined. One of the difficulties in bringing together the beliefs of a successful method of self-help therapy and the scientific tradition of questioning and analysing ideas is that the beliefs will be weakened. Although the concepts may not provide a completely accurate picture of addiction and its cure, belief in them is essential as a way of helping residents to make sense of their experience. The same applies to many self-help movements and it is important that professionals working with them appreciate this (Antze 1979).

More tangible problems have also occurred in the working relationships between professional and ex-addict staff. Ex-addicts lack the general social status and salaries of qualified professionals, and although much has been done in some countries to create a career structure for ex-addicts there remains a wide gap in the career opportunities of professional and ex-addicts, unless the latter are able to make the move into mainstream professional work. Otherwise they may still feel with justification that they are treated as second-class professionals, trapped in a role which confers on them a non-transferable status.

CULTURAL BREAKTHROUGH OR CULT?

In his book *Daytop Village* sociologist Barry Sugarman (1974) claims that concept houses have managed to combine two conflicting aspects of American and Western culture. One is the 'Protestant Ethic' – 'the notion that man should strive to overcome any obstacles to his ambitions lying either in the physical environment or within himself. The other is altruism, showing concern for others, which has 'always been a major element in the Judaeo-Christian humanist tradition'. Sugarman points out that these two values, ambition and concern for others, are usually in opposition to one another. In an almost unique way, he says, concept-based therapeutic communities have 'brought together the emphasis on mastery of one's own life situation and the value of altruism, an achievement of profoundly important implications, which explains the fascination that Synanon, Daytop, etc., have exercised over many visitors.' Cultural breakthrough!

Yet Synanon itself also came to exemplify another feature of American culture: the existence of numerous sects and cults of a religious or semi-religious nature. The background to Synanon is of interest here (Glaser 1977). Dederich and the other founders of Synanon were all members of Alcoholics Anonymous and many features of AA were carried over into the new organization. Alcoholics Anonymous, like Synanon, fosters an intense feeling of fellowship between members through the open discussion of personal histories and problems. It offers a clear series of steps to follow to recovery, and gives the recovered alcoholic the identity of a valued person who can help others. A major influence on Alcoholics Anonymous, and through it on Synanon and the concept-based therapeutic communities, was a movement known as the Oxford Group. This was a religious movement devoted to spiritual rebirth founded at the beginning of the twentieth century by a young American Lutheran minister, Frank Buchman. (The connection with Oxford seems tenuous. Buchman reported having had a mystical experience in the English town of Keswick, and later having taught near Oxford.) The Oxford Group grew to become an international organization, changing its name to the First Christian Fellowship and then in 1938 to Moral Rearmament. Under this name it became linked to the United States' crusade against communism in the 1950s, the infamous McCarthy era. Rather less has been heard of it of late.

From our point of view the interest of the Oxford Group lies in some of its principles, which foreshadowed those of concept-based therapeutic communities. These included the open confession of misdeeds in group meetings, atoning for misdeeds by making restitution to those you have wronged, dramatic conversion to a new set of convictions which guarantee a trouble-free future, and accepting guidance for all one's actions from the divinely inspired authority of the leader. In many ways this is the stuff of all evangelical sects. The Oxford Group's distinguishing feature, which it imparted to Alcoholics Anonymous and Synanon, was the practice of group confession of personal failure, and total openness and honesty between group members.

Synanon started as a therapeutic community, but came increasingly to resemble its predecessor, the Oxford Group. In so doing it changed from a therapeutic community to a religious cult community.

DIFFERENCES BETWEEN CULTS AND THERAPEUTIC COMMUNITIES

This raises the question of what the differences are between a cult community and a therapeutic one. There are sufficient similarities to give some grounds for confusion between the two. Both are often started and led by someone with personal 'charisma'; both claim to help those who feel psychologically and socially inadequate; both seek to create in their members a high level of commitment to the community; and both operate in some degree of isolation from the outside world.

The differences are in the *aims* of the community, the *contract* – what is offered to members and expected in return – and the way *control* is exercised.

The aim of many cult communities is to establish an ideal lifestyle in which negative human qualities such as greed or jealousy disappear. Some may actively seek to convert others to this way of life, to 'spread the gospel'. In contrast, the aims of a therapeutic community are concerned primarily with establishing a culture in which individual change is possible. Complete solutions are not offered. Residents are expected to leave eventually, having learned to cope better with the many problems they still have to face.

In a cult community, members are typically promised a complete and lasting solution to life's problems in return for complete acceptance of the cult's philosophy and practices. In a therapeutic community, rules and expectations do not require total and immediate acceptance – indeed this would be antitherapeutic – but are regarded as a testing ground for the resident's subsequent relationships with authority and society.

In a cult community, leadership and decisions about the community are usually not openly discussed, and may often be determined by a single person or small group whose authority is not open to question. By contrast in a therapeutic community, decisions may or may not be taken democratically by the whole community, according to the kind of therapeutic community it is, but can be freely discussed and challenged in group meetings.

What safeguards are there against a therapeutic community developing into a cult? The lessons of Synanon suggest that at heart what is needed is to maintain an openness to people and ideas from outside the community, to listen to and meet critics rather than regard them as enemies. There is also a need to allow debate within the community, so that established ideas and ways of doing things can be questioned, not to have to speak with one voice in an effort to preserve harmony at any price. To do this is to maintain what

Tom Main called a culture of enquiry. This is achieved both through the personal commitment to it of the leaders in the community, and through regular meetings in which staff roles and the way decisions are made and authority is exercised can be regularly examined and questioned. In effect this is to suggest that *all* therapeutic communities need to have an effective element of democratic functioning at the staff level, at least.

CHAPTER 8

Anti-Psychiatry and Alternative Asylum

Individuals in need of psychological help or refuge have not always turned for help to psychiatry and its allied professions. Religious communities have provided alternative care for the psychologically disabled for many centuries. The first was probably at Geel in Belgium, which became a special place of pilgrimage for 'lunatics' in the fourteenth century (Parry-Jones 1981). In recent times communities for the mentally handicapped and for maladjusted children have been established by several Christian organizations. The best known of these are probably associated with the work of Rudolf Steiner, the Austrian teacher–philosopher who created a movement known as Anthroposophy. He established a number of educational principles which, although rather different from those of most therapeutic communities, are today applied in a number of schools and communities whose aims are similar. An example is the international network of Camphill Village Communities for mentally handicapped children and adults. These communities and others, such as L'Arche (Vanier 1982), provide a home for many people who would otherwise often be in state institutions of one sort or another. Although such communities bear an obvious similarity to other therapeutic communities – valuing the open expression of feelings, the development of personal relationships, and the equal sharing of daily tasks – in other respects they differ from them. There is relatively little emphasis on the use of groups for therapeutic purposes and relatively little exploration of conflicts between members or of the unconscious and defensive aspects of relationships.

Until the 1960s, religious communities of one kind or another were probably the only alternative to psychiatric institutions for people who needed a healing environment away from everyday society. Since then there has been a huge growth in the number of non-professional self-help groups and organizations for people suffering from many kinds of physical, psychological and social disabilities. Concept-based therapeutic communities, described in the previous chapter, belong to this growth, which reflected the much wider social changes which took place in the 1960s. This was the decade in which established authority in many forms – medicine, education, the police, politicians – came under popular attack. It was the decade of flower power and student protest, of alternative lifestyles in communes and religious sects, of alternative therapies such as meditation, LSD, and encounter groups. Within this social climate there emerged a number of 'causes célèbres': one was anti-psychiatry.

'Anti-psychiatry' was the name given to a view of psychiatry which became a kind of crusade in the late 1960s and early 1970s. Although its direct influence on mental health services has always been marginal, it became a touchstone – a source of what to believe – for many people working in the field of mental health, in particular for those who worked in therapeutic communities. Today its influence is probably most apparent in the survivor and user movements (Johnstone 1989, Campbell 1996, Read and Reynolds 1996) and in the continuing debates within the mental health professions concerning the nature of mental illness and the role of professionals (Smail 1988, Boyle 1996, Barker and Davidson 1996).

The chief concern of anti-psychiatry was with beliefs and ideas: about the nature of mental illness, about the role of psychiatrists and psychiatry, about what constitutes 'normal' behaviour in society. But anti-psychiatry gave rise also to a number of practical projects intended to help those who were actual or potential psychiatric patients. Among these projects were small communities and households which provided an alternative form of asylum to psychiatric hospitals. In some respects they were the first to take therapeutic community principles and extend them beyond the walls, and the limitations, of the psychiatric hospital. Today the revolutionary nature of these households has been lessened by the general move away from hospital-based therapies, but they remain at the far end of the therapeutic community spectrum from the highly structured concept-based communities, tending to have as little structure as possible. More than the other types of therapeutic communities described in this book, those which emerged from the anti-psychiatry movement were the product of ideas rather than chance combinations of circumstances. They were conscious attempts to put into practice the theories of their founders. To understand them, therefore, we have to understand the ideas behind them.

THE BASIC IDEAS

In 1967 two British psychiatrists, Ronald Laing and David Cooper, both published books which launched a vehement attack on conventional hospital-based psychiatry, in particular on the treatment of patients labelled as schizophrenic. Cooper's book, *Psychiatry and Anti-Psychiatry* (1967), gave the new movement its name, and Laing's *Politics of Experience* (1967) became required reading for a generation of young people for whom 'inner experience' was elevated to a way of life, commemorated in Timothy Leary's famous slogan 'turn on, tune in, drop out'. A year either side of 1967, a French psychoanalyst, Jacques Lacan, and an Italian psychiatrist, Franco Basaglia, also published books which became landmarks in an international anti-psychiatry movement (Ingleby 1981). In the United States the psychoanalyst Thomas Szasz published a string of books in the 1960s and 1970s with such resounding titles as *The Myth of Mental Illness* and *The Manufacture of Madness*. What were all these doctors saying?

Despite their differences they were all concerned with a common dilemma: 'whose side is the psychiatrist on'? Is his job to help the patient become a whole, healthy autonomous individual, or is it to preserve the social peace by getting patients to fit in with the way others want them to be? Does he serve the patient or society?

The problem was not new. Freud was well aware of it, and any psychiatrist or social worker who has had to decide whether to admit a patient to hospital against his will has had to face it. A conventional way out of the dilemma has been to include the patient's resistance to treatment as one of the symptoms of his illness – a strategy roundly condemned by the anti-psychiatrists. If the patient's unwillingness to be treated is not seen as part of the illness, the rights and wrongs of the situation become harder to judge, and the psychiatrist may feel he is being put in the role of jailer or policeman if he forces the patient to have treatment.

In response to such ethical problems the anti-psychiatrists had little doubt. Their responsibility was to the patient only. They were not there to be jailers or policemen, to persuade the patient to behave in a socially acceptable way, or to make life easier for the patient's relatives or society in general. They were there to help people who were temporarily overwhelmed by life's difficulties, to guide them through the turmoil of their breakdown till they found their way again. Some anti-psychiatrists rejected completely the idea of mental illness. They saw it as a concept with little intrinsic value, only useful as a justification for giving patients treatments they didn't want to have. Most accepted that peculiar states of mind, which we call madness or psychosis, do exist, but that these states provide no reason for ostracizing people or taking control over their lives. Some emphasized the need to make special provision for people experiencing such states of mind, so that they could go through them without interference. Others stressed the need for active efforts to deal with the problems that produced the breakdown by working in the setting where it first arose – the family and the neighbourhood.

These views led anti-psychiatrists to withdraw from practising psychiatry in conventional settings, because they would inevitably be on the side of society, or at least caught between conflicting interests. Psychiatric hospitals in particular were seen as beyond any hope of real improvement, too tainted by their function of holding people against their will, or simply by their institutional codes of conduct which inhibited the spontaneity and autonomy of staff and patients alike. To the anti-psychiatrists even therapeutic communities could not offer real freedom from these constraints as long as they were based in hospitals. The staff in hospital-based therapeutic communities were often prepared to tolerate these limitations, or try to change them from within. The anti-psychiatrists were not. They were critical not only of hospitals but of psychotherapists who pursued goals of social adjustment and conformity with their patients, rather than using therapy purely as a means to greater self-knowledge and autonomy.

In addition to this central concern about the role of the psychiatrist and the goals of psychiatric treatment, two related issues were of vital importance to anti-psychiatry: the true nature of what we call schizophrenia, and the relationship between mental illness and the way society itself functions.

An important idea in the setting up of alternative asylums was that psychosis – schizophrenia in particular – was not an illness to be cured but a remarkable inner journey to be guided through. The schizophrenic was someone who, without wishing to, had embarked on a voyage back to his earliest experiences and his inner self. Once embarked, what he needed was the presence of others who could look after him and guide him through the experience until he returned 'reborn', as it were. Evidence for this heroic view of schizophrenia was found in the way similar experiences were treated in other cultures and other periods of history: healing rituals had often involved a kind of spiritual journey and rebirth. Laing wrote:

> under all circumstances a man may get stuck, lose himself, and have to turn round and go back a long way to find himself again. Only under certain socio-economic conditions (i.e. present-day Western society) will he be said to suffer from schizophrenia. (Laing 1971)

The implication of this view was that psychiatric treatments like drugs and ECT actually prevented recovery, since they stopped the journey. What was needed was some special provision, a place where people could go to have a breakdown. This suggestion had earlier been put forward by the eminent British psychoanalyst Donald Winnicott, one of Laing's supervisors, and it led to the setting up of Kingsley Hall, the first anti-psychiatry community, which is described below.

Here is not the place to evaluate the treatment of schizophrenia. Its nature, causes and cures are still the subject of debate within psychiatry (Boyle

1990, 1996). Yet there is evidence that for some people who experience a psychotic breakdown, in which for a while they become helpless and dependent on others, the anti-psychiatry approach may enable them to recover without physical treatment (McGlashen and Levy 1977, Berke 1979, Mosher and Burti 1994).

The anti-psychiatrists' view of the relationship between mental illness and society also takes us into realms which are beyond the scope of this book to explore in depth. Briefly, there are two arguments. One, particularly associated with the work of Laing, states that living in modern Western society is so damaging to our true spontaneous natures that becoming 'mentally ill' may actually be a healthier response than staying 'normal'. The other argument, more political and associated with the writings of Marxist psychiatrists such as Cooper and the French anti-psychiatrists, is that those who are called mentally ill are the victims of a conspiracy by society to deny the truth of what they are saying. The patient's illness is seen as a social or political protest, and psychiatric treatment is equated with political repression. Both arguments have a point, and there is no doubt that the second was literally true in some countries, such as the former Soviet Union. How far you go along with these arguments depends largely on your own political view of the world.

In its style and rhetoric anti-psychiatry appeals to those looking for an anti-establishment ideology to believe in. Shorn of its poetry and politics it loses some of its attractiveness but contains ideas which have nevertheless had a pronounced effect on conventional psychiatry. Techniques of crisis intervention, family therapy and psychosocial intervention, the growing influence of users on the provision of mental health services, and indeed the whole programme of hospital closures described in Chapter 6, have been influenced by the anti-psychiatrists' views on the damaging effects of institutional life, on the importance of listening to the experience of the psychotic individual, and on the rights of people suffering from mental illness to be given equal respect and opportunities as other members of society.

Yet to point to the ways in which anti-psychiatry has influenced the practice of conventional psychiatry risks missing what it was really about, for it was and remains much more about beliefs and values than about practical ways of doing things. It was an attempt to extend our view of psychological 'breakdown' to include its spiritual, social and political dimensions. It pointed out that the concept of 'illness' was far too restricting to enable us fully to understand madness, and reminded us that psychiatrists now deal with the problems that were once the domain of priests. While modern psychotropic drugs can sometimes offer speedy relief to those in serious mental distress, there may be some for whom other healing processes are more appropriate. No doubt the anti-psychiatrists overstated their case when they claimed that only they understood the 'truth' about madness and that their approach was best for everyone. Yet their exaggerated claims were perhaps an indication of the extent to which it seemed that these other dimensions of mental illness had been previously neglected.

The therapeutic community pioneers in the 1940s and 1950s had set themselves the target of trying to change psychiatry from within – with some success. The anti-psychiatrists of the 1960s and 1970s went a stage further and proposed that a radical alternative to the psychiatric establishment was needed. The first and still perhaps the best-known attempt to put this proposal into practice was Kingsley Hall.

ANTI-PSYCHIATRY IN PRACTICE
Villa 21: A Failed Experiment

In the early 1960s David Cooper experimented in taking a therapeutic community in a psychiatric hospital beyond the usual limits of tolerance for nonconformity. Patients in Villa 21 at Shenley Hospital were free to get up when they chose and attend as much or as little of the daily programme as they chose. Staff restricted the exercise of their authority to the minimum possible, on the assumption that patients would eventually take responsibility for themselves. The experiment did not last very long. The hospital authorities became increasingly critical of the state of the ward, and the staff's anxieties mounted along with the piles of unwashed plates. In Cooper's absence the staff decided to reimpose certain expectations about attendance at meetings and the length of leave patients could take. (It is interesting that untidiness and leave-taking were two of the issues that also confronted Bion in his original attempt to get patients to take collective responsibility. In his case he was successful with the patients but not with the hospital authorities.) Cooper accepted the staff's decision to reassert their authority. He saw this as confirmation that in a hospital it was inevitable that staff would feel too concerned about the opinions of their colleagues and supervisors to let such an experiment succeed – as he believed it would if it went on long enough. He believed that a true experiment in allowing patients complete freedom and autonomy in running their lives could only take place outside the hospital (Cooper 1967).

Kingsley Hall: A Seminal Five-year Experiment

Kingsley Hall was a large community centre built around the turn of the century in the heart of London's working-class East End. It had been used for many pioneering projects to help poor people, and the trustees were sympathetic to Laing and his colleagues, who were looking for somewhere to put into practice their ideas about an alternative to psychiatric hospitals. In 1965 they agreed to lend Kingsley Hall to the Philadelphia Association, which had been formed by Laing and his colleagues. Between then and 1970, when the lease ran out, 119 people stayed at the Hall. Most stayed for no longer than six months, but a few stayed for a year or more. One of those who stayed longer was Mary Barnes, whose written account of her profound regression to passive helplessness and eventual recovery made her one of the celebrities of anti-psychiatry and a key figure in the argument for the Kingsley Hall approach. Mary Barnes was one of those – about a third of the residents – who had previously been treated as a psychiatric in-patient. Others had been out-patients, and about a third had no psychiatric history. Many of these were qualified or trainee psychiatrists and psychotherapists, who wanted to take part in this experiment in 'unlabelled' living. Of the fifteen to twenty-five people living in Kingsley Hall at any one time, only three or four were actually psychotic (Laing 1971, Berke 1980).

What was Kingsley Hall like? When I visited there in the late 1960s, I was struck by the run-down appearance of the place, both outside and inside. Graffiti in the living room denounced conventional psychiatric treatments – such as the drug Largactil. Individuals had their own rooms where they were free to spend as much time as they wanted. Some rooms were in a fairly squalid condition. One was liberally decorated with the droppings of a pet bird. Joseph Berke, a psychiatrist who lived in Kingsley Hall, described the way it worked as follows:

> People who were psychotic were given space, they were given company if they wished, or not, and they were given a great deal of physical support if necessary. It was a feature about life at Kingsley Hall that as people were not considered ill, they did not have to be treated. No drugs were given to anybody. There were no staff and no patients, and there was no formal structure of doing things around the Hall, yet things got done. There were people who were 'up' and people who were 'down'. The people who were 'up' or capable of functioning in a more usual social sense look after the Hall. (Berke 1980)

How people joined, how things got done, and the absence of 'staff' and 'patient' roles, were also discussed by Morton Schatzman:

> If someone wishes to live at Kingsley Hall he must meet some or all of the residents first. Sometimes they invite him to stay for an evening meal or a weekend. The residents ask those people to join the community whom they like or whom they feel would benefit at Kingsley Hall or both. The residents consider it best for a balance to exist between those who are free to deal with ordinary social and economic needs – to shop for food, wash dishes, scrub floors, clean toilets, stoke the furnace, repair broken fuses, and pay the bills – and those who cannot or choose not to be, and wish to work upon themselves ... No one who lives at Kingsley Hall sees those

who perform work upon the external material world as 'staff', and those who do not as 'patients'. No caste system forbids people to move freely from one sub-group to another, as it does in mental hospitals. (Shatzman 1969)

Mary Barnes' story illustrates both the possibilities of success and some of the difficulties and risks involved in the anti-psychiatrists' approach. Before coming to Kingsley Hall in her forties she had been diagnosed as schizophrenic and had had several periods of hospitalization, although she had also been able to work successfully as a nurse in between them, and had achieved the position of nurse tutor. She shared Laing's views on schizophrenia, and was herself seeking the opportunity to experience a complete breakdown without having it treated. The fact that she was able to 'hold on' for a year or so until Kingsley Hall was opened suggests that she had considerable personal resources. Initially she continued in her job while living at Kingsley Hall, but then resigned and allowed herself to regress, without any external or internal inhibitions. Later she wrote, 'I tore off my clothes, feeling I had to be naked, lay on the floor with my shits and water, smeared the walls with faeces. Was wild and noisy about the house or sitting in a heap on the kitchen floor.' Schatzman, there at the same time, wrote that: 'others found it difficult to live with her when she smeared faeces on her body and on the walls of her room. Her room was next to the kitchen and the odour came through the wall.'

Mary Barnes took to lying in her bed all day and refusing food. It was at this stage that the anti-psychiatry belief in non-interference, in giving people total freedom to live as they chose, came under a severe test. Joseph Berke writes that he was horrified when he arrived at Kingsley Hall after an absence to discover that she was so 'thin that it was felt that she couldn't even be sent to hospital, as we might be prosecuted for keeping a person like that'. An intense debate took place between Laing and his colleagues, at which it was recognized that either the principle of complete self-responsibility would have to be sacrificed, or Mary Barnes might die. Laing accepted the point and told her that he wanted her to eat (Blake, personal communication). Berke began to feed her, like a baby, with milk from a bottle. Others took turns at looking after her, and gradually she began the long and tortuous journey back to mental and physical health. As part of this recovery she expressed her feelings in dozens of huge vivid paintings. She and Joseph Berke wrote a joint book about her experiences at Kingsley Hall, which also became the subject of a play (Barnes and Berke 1971).

Although Mary Barnes was to become the best known of Kingsley Hall's residents, she was almost certainly not typical. Few went through such an extreme and protracted period of 'working on themselves'. Probably more typical were several whom Schatzman (1969) interviewed and described.

They were people who in various ways were in a state of personal conflict and stalemate. They resented having to conform to other people's expectations, but found it impossible in ordinary life to be assertive, aggressive, selfish or rude, in a word, to rebel. Since there were so few expectations at Kingsley Hall about what was normal social behaviour and no rules to conform to, these people could start to do things they would never have dared to do outside. Here they could decide what they wanted to do, when they wanted to do it, and be only as pleasant and sociable as they felt. The anti-psychiatry principle of not telling people what to do gave them the freedom they needed to find their own identity. It is likely that Kingsley Hall, although set up to help those going through a psychotic breakdown, was more often of help to young people such as these.

After Kingsley Hall

In its five years as a living experiment in anti-psychiatry, many psychiatrists and other professionals had come to Kingsley Hall to experience the approach at first hand. When it closed in 1970 some decided to continue its work elsewhere. In England two new projects were started as alternatives to psychiatric hospitals. Leon Redler formed the Archway Community, in a collection of run-down houses in north London. This later became part of the Philadelphia Association, which has founded some twenty therapeutic community households since then and presently has three, all in London. A second group, including Joseph Berke and Morton Schatzman, started the Arbours Association which established a Crisis Centre and three long-term communities in London. Both associations also offer a full training in psychotherapy, the Arbours using residential placements in their communities as part of the training.

The communities are usually small, housing perhaps six to ten people, with an atmosphere of laissez-faire permissiveness. Residents can involve themselves in as much or as little of the communal life of the house as they wish, although they are expected to share responsibility for the day-to-day running of the household and to attend group meetings held two or three times a week. The emphasis is on coming to terms with oneself, usually aided by individual psychotherapy outside the community, more than on social learning through group involvement. The community is seen as a 'place to be', somewhere that offers 'the reassurance of the ordinary', rather than as an instrument of therapy.

Two projects are of particular interest. One is the Arbours Crisis Centre, which has developed a synthesis of crisis intervention, psychotherapy and temporary sanctuary (Berke *et al.* 1995). A team of therapists, some of whom live in the centre, deal with letters and phone calls from people in emotional crises and offer what help they think is needed. This can be talking on the telephone, meeting people in their home, regular individual or family therapy, or offering an individual or a family a place to stay for a few weeks or months. The therapists believe that with these facilities most levels of disturbance, including acute psychosis, can be contained and worked with without the use of medication. In the centre itself, a comfortable, attractively decorated house in north London, there is little pressure on individuals to conform. The therapists look after the house and are available round the clock for informal conversations. Formal meetings are held several times a week with those closely involved in the crisis. It is a condition of offering someone accommodation that all those people involved in the crisis are willing to be involved in these meetings. The therapists are concerned to avoid the situation, which often happens with admission to a psychiatric hospital, where a crisis is resolved by one person being defined as ill. No one is defined as a patient: all are the 'guests' of the resident therapists. They believe that by providing whatever amount of support and understanding is needed, the crisis can be contained, the people involved can be calmed, and the reasons for the crisis can be gone into and resolved. By providing the range of facilities it does, the Crisis Centre goes beyond anti-psychiatry and in some ways provides a model for a non-hospital based alternative psychiatric service. There is much in Arbours' approach that is consistent with the current emphasis on Community Care, as its Service Specification makes clear.

In the United States a number of projects also took shape building on the work at Kingsley Hall. One of these, Soteria, combined the anti-psychiatrists' belief in the self-healing possibilities of certain psychotic states, with an acceptance of the value of careful research into the success of such a venture when compared with conventional treatment. Soteria ran for twelve years in a large comfortable house in San Francisco, with accommodation for six young schizophrenic patients with six staff working shifts. In some ways Soteria resembled the hospital-based therapeutic communities described earlier in this book. The major differences were: (a) its small size and homely setting which made possible more intimacy and cohesiveness than in most hospitals; (b) the relative absence of staff control or imposed structure; and (c) the attempt to rely on the self-healing nature of psychosis. The attitude concerning medication was not dogmatic, however, and drugs were given to those patients – relatively few – who showed no change after six weeks. Comparing Soteria with conventional in-patient treatments it was found that Soteria patients not only did better but were more likely to make the positive step of leaving the parental home (Mosher et al. 1975).

THE LEGACY OF ANTI-PSYCHIATRY

Thirty years after Kingsley Hall and the peak of interest in the ideas of R.D. Laing and his colleagues, it can be argued that anti-psychiatry has left little trace in the approach of the medical profession to mental illness or distress. Our society – which means most of us, most of the time – looks for a painless fix to its problems, and psychiatry has been able to oblige with new medications such as Prozac, which promise to banish unwanted emotional states without any need to engage with the problems behind the symptoms. But while it is probably true that the medical profession has not shifted a great deal (perhaps because as a society we don't want it to), the attempt to pull what we call mental illness away from being seen as predominately a medical problem located in one individual, towards seeing it as an interpersonal, communication problem located in a social context (family and society), is an attempt that has continued to make headway. But while the early anti-psychiatrists were all psychiatrists themselves, those who pursue this attempt now tend to come from a background in clinical psychology, psychiatric nursing or social work, or from outside the professions, including those with first-hand experience of mental breakdown.

In fact this way of seeing mental disorder has a long tradition. It can be seen in the approach of the Quakers when creating what came to be called Moral Treatment in the early nineteenth century (see Chapter 2) and the early asylum pioneers; it inspired the educationalists who created therapeutic communities for children in the 1930s (see Chapter 3); Foulkes, in developing group analysis in the 1940s, went so far as to describe the concept of the individual as a 'plausible abstraction' and saw the focus of treatment as the communication between the individual and the group (Pines 1983). What was new in anti-psychiatry was explicitly linking this view to a debate about social and political values.

The continued headway being made by an anti-psychiatry view of mental disorder is perhaps most evident in the attention given to the experiences and the rights of those who are treated by mental health professionals.

Croft and Beresford have commented in their regular 'user views' column in the journal *Changes* on the achievements of the psychiatric system survivors' movement in the UK over the last fifteen years:

> There are now local, regional, national and international organisations of survivors ranging from patients' councils in hospitals to community-based self-advocacy, support and campaigning groups. Survivors have developed their own user-led training, emancipatory research, independent consultancy and user-led alternatives, as well as their own writing and arts… Little of this could have been imagined or expected just twenty years ago (Croft and Bereseford 1997).

However, they also point out that a lot of this progress has depended for support on statutory organizations that do things *for* those who use mental health services, and contrast this with the autonomy of the self-help movement for people with physical disabilities. Taken more broadly the growth of self-help organizations for people with a range of afflictions, disabilities and minority concerns has been one of the major social trends in the last third of the twentieth century. (For an excellent early account of successful self-help movements see Lieberman *et al.* (1979).) From this broad perspective anti-psychiatry was one aspect of the sea change in attitudes towards traditional sources of authority in society in the 1960s, and the present users/survivors movement is one aspect of the settling down of that sea change into a philosophy or ideology of what we might term victim empowerment. Such an ideology carries with it risks as well as opportunities for recognition and achievement. Hinshelwood (1997) has described the way any ideology can fool its followers into false certainties and blind them to other points of view, leading to the rejection of all criticism. Indeed therapeutic communities themselves have at times shared this fate of idealization (Hobson 1979).

The present-day influence of the anti-psychiatry movement can be seen in other ways too.

- The continuation and growth of alternative forms of support or sanctuary for those who want to avoid the medicalization of their emotional distress. Alongside the continuing work of the Arbours and Philadelphia Associations is the growth in the employment of counsellors in primary care, in the field of complementary therapies and in therapies that emphasize the spiritual and transpersonal aspects of experience.

- The availability of psychotherapy trainings with an anti-psychiatry orientation ensures a continuing influence through the trainees who subsequently take up employment in the health services or voluntary sector. Some trainings, such as the Arbours, include the experience of living in a therapeutic community household for several months.

- The popularity of the writings of well-known psychotherapists who reject the medicalization of complex social-emotional problems, such as Susie Orbach (1994), Dorothy Rowe (1995) and David Smail (1988).

- The recent widely reviewed book reappraising R.D. Laing's work and influence by Kotowicz (1997).

No doubt a majority of people will continue to place their reliance in doctors when threatened with the chaos and anxiety of serious mental disorder, since doctors are felt, like parents, to 'know what to do' in times of crisis. And most doctors will continue to place their reliance in forms of treatment they know and understand – drugs, practical advice, reassurance, and so on. The approach is simple – seeing the problem as exclusively located in a particular individual – and offers opportunities for action, both attractive at times of stress. The alternative approach is to get people to share responsibility for understanding the situation and to engage with others in looking for solutions. This approach operates in another dimension: the interpersonal, the effects people have on one another. The assumption that this is the main dimension in which psychological disorders occur, and where the work of putting them right must take place, is not one that has been generally accepted in our society.

CHAPTER 9

The Future of Therapeutic Communities[1]

When the first edition of this book was published there was a widely held view that therapeutic communities had been in decline since the 1970s. Manning (1976) had charted their progress in terms of the general pattern of growth and decline of social movements. He had identified therapeutic communities as being near the end point where a movement becomes stagnant and bureaucratic. Clark (1977) had written that 'by the 1970s most psychiatrists were able to snuggle back into their nineteenth century identities and dismiss the therapeutic community as a fad'. Well, the therapeutic community *movement* may have died, but clearly therapeutic communities themselves have not. Indeed they may be enjoying something of a comeback having undergone a transformation from the status of a crusade to humanize the atmosphere of the old mental hospitals to a recognized and effective method of treatment or care for particular kinds of disorder. But while therapeutic communities and the ideas behind them are still alive, they remain vulnerable to a number of pressures.

In the UK, where most are funded (directly or indirectly) out of the public purse, therapeutic communities have been squeezed very tightly by the changes in health care management and there have been some significant casualties as well as some near misses. At the same time much of the thinking within the user participation movement and the efforts of organizations that represent the consumers of mental health services and their carers, contain strong elements of the original therapeutic community ideas.

In thinking about the place of therapeutic communities in future mental health services I have organized my ideas around three questions.

---

1 This chapter is based on a paper given by the author to the Windsor conference in 1993 (Kennard 1994).

(1)   What are the essential, defining characteristics that have been clustered together under the umbrella of the therapeutic community that can provide a distinctive and useful way of thinking about any task-centred setting?

(2)   How have the changes in economic, ideological and professional priorities over the past twenty years affected the relevance of this way of working, and how far can it be adapted to meet these changes without losing what makes it distinctive?

(3)   What are the ways forward?

SOME DEFINING CHARACTERISTICS

I have found it useful to set out in Figure 9.1 the defining characteristics in a way that shows the different tiers of the therapeutic community concept. At the top are the most general or common situations found in many organizations. The first three may be found in many small good working teams of various kinds. Level 4 brings in the kind of therapeutic community envisaged in Maxwell Jones' key phrase, a living learning situation, and can be found in many good rehabilitation units even where the therapeutic community label is not applied. The next two levels introduce Tom Main's recognition of the therapeutic community as a tool for the investigation of interpersonal processes, or as he termed it, a culture of enquiry. This now becomes a quite highly developed form of the concept. The last level refers to the structural requirements for any of this to take place but which are especially necessary at the higher levels.

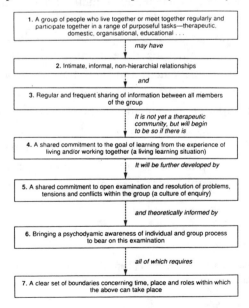

Figure 9.1 Defining characteristics of the therapeutic community concept

Thinking about the therapeutic community in this way can help us to see that its more basic elements are present in many non-therapeutic enterprises, such as schools and other educational institutions, small businesses (especially those run as collectives), larger organizations which delegate to semi-autonomous units, and groups that come together to campaign or organize for a particular goal.

I will take it as accepted for the purpose of this book that this set of activities, whatever we call them, has obvious advantages in the fields of psychotherapy, rehabilitation, education and management. Now to the second question, which I will approach under three headings.

THE QUESTION OF COST

When used as a form of long-term residential treatment with a team of qualified staff, a therapeutic community is expensive. This may not have mattered in a period of economic growth, but in times of economic stringency and public sector cuts, therapeutic communities are vulnerable. Can the concept be applied more cheaply without loss of quality? Can it be applied outside the public sector or without state funds? Here are two examples, from outside the United Kingdom.

Von Wallenberg Pachaly (1992) has described a time-limited psychotherapeutic community that meets for between ten and twenty-eight days once or twice a year. Its members are chosen from the weekly out-patient psychotherapy groups run by the members of a weekly supervision group, who select patients who can benefit from a brief intensification of their psychotherapy. The author's description suggests that this is a carefully thought-out and structured situation with enormous learning potential both for staff and patients. Costs are kept as low as possible – DM80 (£30) a day in 1992. Patients, most of whom are in work, are responsible for finding their own funding.

Markezinis *et al.* (1992) from the Open Psychotherapeutic Centre in Athens has described a therapeutic community that meets for just one day a fortnight so that people can attend while maintaining a job or living at a long distance, and who have limited financial means. Although only meeting twice a month, a sense of community was created through participation in a number of different formal and informal activities together, and prospective members have a trial period as they would in any residential or daily therapeutic community. In fact there are two communities that meet on alternate weeks. Although members are expected to pay for themselves, a range of options are available for those unable to do so, such as contributing a particular skill or hobby to the community through setting up a group for other members. The cost per day (10,000 drachmas = £28 in 1992) was around twice the cost of a day in a state psychiatric hospital and half the cost of a day in a general hospital psychiatric unit. (Comparing average lengths of treatment in each setting, twenty-four months attending the fortnightly therapeutic community cost £1352, three and a half months in a psychiatric hospital cost £1682 and one and a half months in a general hospital unit cost £2532. While we might need to triple or quadruple these figures to obtain their UK equivalent it is clear that the fortnightly therapeutic community model represents a cheaper option than in-patient care.) What is particularly interesting is that the authors report that this format was able to sustain quite disturbed patients at home, and that the two-week break between each community day seemed to increase the effect of the therapy. The model of an intensive therapeutic community experienced one day a fortnight has many interesting implications, in terms of cost, maintaining people in their own homes and jobs, and offering services to a wide geographical area.

THE SHIFT OF HEALTH CARE INTO THE COMMUNITY

Therapeutic communities were first 'grown' in hospitals, their natural soil. To continue the analogy, most long-stay patients have been turfed out into the wider community and the staff who worked with them dispersed. Although, as we have seen in earlier chapters, many therapeutic communities exist in smaller non-hospital settings, there has been a loss of the creative momentum of a critical mass of staff that hospitals provided. Seen from the present-day perspective the early therapeutic community pioneers may have accepted too readily the inevitability of most long-term care being hospital based. What remains to be seen is whether community-based care in its various manifestations can produce the same cohesion and creativity among colleagues that led to the creation of such remarkable innovations within the psychiatric hospitals. It depends a lot on the next topic.

CHANGING PROFESSIONAL IDEOLOGIES

What were the ideologies that supported, or were around at the time of, the early therapeutic communities? The 1950s and especially the 1960s were associated with antipathy towards traditional sources of authority – parents, politicians, teachers, the police, the medical profession – with the breaking down of social conventions, with explorations in social intimacy in encounter groups and in the new permissive lifestyle, with sit-ins and love-ins.

Therapeutic communities with their role blurring, group culture and egalitarian relationships were much in tune with these new social frontiers. Where are the frontiers today? What are the ideologies that shape us today as citizens and as professional caregivers? I think the following can be identified.

There is the *entrepreneurial culture* with its priorities of cost-effectiveness and organizational leanness, and its redefinition of us all as providers and customers engaged in the marketing of products to each other. Although with the change to a Labour government this culture may have passed its peak, the momentum created will be with us for some time to come.

There is the emphasis on the *centrality of the individual* and, within the health and social services, on *individual* care plans and care managers. While this is an understandable and appropriate reaction to the old institutional-ized practice of treating everyone the same, taken to an extreme (and I think it often is) the interaction *between* individuals, whether in a family or group home or hospital ward or day centre or wherever, is simply ignored. There is no frame to put it in, so to speak, and as staff are allocated as key workers to individual clients or patients, there is usually no one left whose role it is to think about the group.

Along with the emphasis on cost-effectiveness and the individual are the twin ideologies of *quality assurance* and *measurable competencies*. The competencies needed to perform not just straightforward practical tasks but the complexities of counselling and psychotherapy are being squared off into separate observable skills that can be rated as present or absent in the work of a practitioner. The ideology is not just applied to staff. Applied to patients/clients it leads to social and personal learning being reduced to a set of skills to be learned: social skills, living skills, assertiveness, anxiety man-agement, anger management and so on. Of course skills and competence are vital components of human life, and their value is noted in Jeff Robert's chapter on training, not least because we are entitled to know that someone providing us with a service, whether therapy or anything else, knows what they are doing. The problem is that this partial view of human relations risks becoming the whole view so that we are nothing more than our performance (Weatherill 1997).

Finally there is the *human rights movement*, which has evolved as the neces-sary antidote to the entrepreneurial culture, to protect *us* as consumers or service users from *us* as exploiters and abusers of power. As psychotherapists and health professionals we have got caught up in the ideological campaign to present all professional care, and especially institutional care, as an imbal-ance of power that almost by definition undermines the individual's right to respect and self-determination (Masson 1989). The search for the holy grail of a non-stigmatized, normal, independent lifestyle for former residents of psychiatric and mental handicap hospitals, under the banner of normaliza-tion, places a wedge between them and the recognition of their need for a so-cially accepting and tolerant (not necessarily normal!) environment.

THE WAY FORWARD

How will therapeutic communities respond to the combined challenge of economic regulation, community-based care, and the new cultural and professional ideologies described above?

Here are some provisional answers:

(1)   As in the examples given earlier, low-cost five-days-a-week (or less) or time-limited therapeutic communities will be developed which have the added advantage of reducing the separation of the individual from his or her home environment.

(2)   The challenge of audit- and evidence-based practice will be accepted. Indeed the therapeutic community's familiarity with user involvement, as it is now called, should make them far less defensive about this than many professionals faced with the same challenge (Campling 1992, Knowles 1992).

(3)   The therapeutic community model will be increasingly taken up within a voluntary sector that is responding to mental health needs with a growing awareness of psychosocial factors, not least because this sector is attracting an increasing number of staff who combine a high level of psychotherapeutic skills with a strong sense of social responsibility. In addition to some of the examples in the mental health field given in previous chapters, two excellent examples of these developments in related fields in the UK are NEWPIN, an organization for single parents, and the Medical Foundation for the Care and Resettlement of Victims of Torture.

(4)   Within community mental health teams, as Cox (1998) has suggested, there is a growing recognition that the emphasis on meeting the needs of individuals must be complemented by some of the core concepts and skills developed in therapeutic communities. These include recognizing potential splits between caregivers and the value of a containing network of relationship, and the vital need for a reflective space for practitioners. Those with direct therapeutic community experience are especially well placed to provide an informed model of such professional practice, either as members of such teams or through teaching, supervision and staff support.

(5)   The loss of the mental hospitals has paradoxically led to an increased emphasis on the need for secure containment for people whose release into the community has led to increased public anxiety, not to mention political embarrassment. Prisons and secure units for those with personality disorders, or who are seen to pose a serious risk to the public, are expanding and in a number of cases are welcoming the therapeutic community concept (Millard 1993). Indeed we have seen

that therapeutic communities of the concept-based type have become 'the treatment of choice' in the American prison system, while the model developed at Grendon in England is likely to be reproduced in new prisons.

Underlying all of these significant developments is the need to respond to the challenge posed by some of the ideologies I have referred to: a blinkered individualism that ignores the social parameters of existence; a view of human rights that excludes certain kinds of human living arrangements; the attempt to present the power imbalance between professional helpers and their clients only in a negative light. These views are one dimensional. Therapeutic community values and practice can be among those forces within society needed to restore the other dimensions to public and professional awareness.

PART II

Working in a Therapeutic Community

Up to this point in the book we have looked at therapeutic communities from the outside, at how they started, what they do and what ideas they use. It is also possible to look at them from the inside. What is it like to be in a therapeutic community, as a resident, a staff member or a student?

A small number of first-hand accounts have been written of the experience of being a resident in a therapeutic community (Barnes and Berke 1971, Mahony 1979, Smith 1981, Matilda 1994) and the reader is encouraged to read these for an insight into what the experience is like. Students on placements have also described their experience (Taggart 1993, Kjartansdottir 1994). The experience of working as a therapist in a therapeutic community is touched on in a good deal of the literature, and some authors have written in very clear, personal terms about their own experience (Greenwood et al. 1994, McAlpin 1996, Burridge 1997).

In this part of the book we look at the experience of being a staff member, from three points of view: the immediate impact of arriving in a therapeutic community, staff roles, and the appropriate training for work in a therapeutic community.

The chapter that follows is an imaginary narrative of three people spending their first day in a therapeutic community. It is imaginary in the sense that the people and the community are fictitious. The background material for the narrative was provided by a number of interviews I had with new staff and trainees in different therapeutic communities, discussing their reactions to their new situation. The community itself is an amalgam of different communities but of necessity had to have a concrete form. I have chosen a hospital-based one because it is the type with which I am most familiar. The newcomers, too, represent a pooling of a wide range of expectations and responses into three, I hope, believable characters.

CHAPTER 10

The First Day

An Imaginary Narrative

Alexander House is a residential psychiatric unit in the grounds of what had once been a large mental hospital and is now the administrative headquarters of the local health authority, as well as housing a number of out-patient services. The patients, or residents, suffer from what are generally referred to as personality disorders. Some have had previous psychiatric admissions and some have had convictions for criminal offences. All are voluntary – i.e. not detained under the Mental Health Act. The staff include the usual psychiatric professions but it will not be immediately apparent who is who in this respect.

Today three newcomers are arriving. Their reasons for coming and their expectations of what it will be like are different.

Sue is training to be a general nurse and likes working with people who are physically ill. However, her training requires her to have experience in working in a psychiatric setting. She has been told that the place she is going to is a therapeutic community, but that means little to her. She's heard from a friend that the staff spend as much time talking about themselves as they do talking about patients, which seems peculiar. But she has an open mind about what to expect and is willing to make the best of it.

Ian is training to be a social worker. He enjoys the group discussions they have on his course and made a point of asking to spend one of his placements in a therapeutic community. Unlike Sue he already knows about them from books and articles, and thinks they are a good thing because they give everyone an equal vote in decision making. Ian doesn't like hierarchies with professionals at the top and clients at the bottom, and he sees therapeutic communities as making a political statement about the rights of those receiving help.

Barbara, unlike Sue and Ian, is not training for a particular occupation. She took a degree in psychology and was then unsure what she wanted to do next. She had a period of feeling depressed and once saw a psychiatrist who referred her to a counsellor. She found this helpful and it led her to become interested in people with emotional problems. She answered an advertisement for a nursing assistant at Alexander House and was invited to come for a day. She has heard a bit about therapeutic communities and is attracted by the idea of staff and residents helping one another.

Let us join Sue, Ian and Barbara as they arrive, as yet unacquainted with one another, at Alexander House. It is 8.20 on a midweek morning. From a distance Alexander House appears set apart from the neighbouring buildings. The 'house' is about the size of a large villa or small hotel. Approaching the building two things catch the eye. There is a broken window on the ground floor, and two young men, one bearded, are sitting on the grass by the entrance. Sue is the first to arrive, and she goes up to them.

'Excuse me, is this Alexander House?'

'Yes, can I help?' answered the man with a beard, not getting up.

'Could you tell me where I could find a member of the staff?'

'Well, I'm a member of staff.'

'I'm sorry,' Sue was taken aback at the man's casual manner although he seemed friendly enough, 'I was told to be here at 8.30. Can you tell me where I should go?'

'That will be for the staff pre-meeting in the green room. The community meeting starts at 9.'

Sue was digesting this information when the other two newcomers arrived.

'Excuse me,' said Ian to Sue, 'I'm starting here today. Could you tell me where the community meeting is?'

This bewildered Sue even more. Was she the only one who hadn't known there was a community meeting?'

'This is my first day too. The community meeting starts at 9, but there's something called a pre-meeting at 8.30.'

'That's right,' said the bearded man, standing up, 'I'm going there now. I'll show you the way if you like.'

'Can I come with you?' asked Barbara.

'My name's Nick,' said the bearded man, and they all introduced themselves.

As they went in, Nick turned to the young man still sitting on the grass.

'Tony, if you want to stay you'll have to explain to the community about why you did that. You know the rules, and I don't see why we should make an exception for you.'

'Crap!' said Tony, not moving from his hunched position.

They went inside and found themselves in a hall with several doors leading off. One or two sleepy-looking people passed them carrying bowls of breakfast cereal. At first sight the inside of the building seemed homely and rather untidy. There were magazines lying around and lots of posters and notices on the walls. It certainly doesn't seem like a hospital, thought Sue. There was no one in sight who looked like a member of staff.

Ian was excited. The casual way they were being introduced made him feel as though they were entering a secret society. He wondered if they were being observed, their reactions being noted. This casual approach is a kind of test, he thought. Barbara trailed behind the others. She would have liked to stay outside and ask Tony what he was angry about. She thought the place looked rather friendly – not like the out-patient clinic she had once attended, with its cold shiny walls and rows of plastic chairs.

They were led through one of the doors and found themselves suddenly in a crowded room. People were sitting on chairs, tables and desks, or helping themselves to coffee from a tray on the floor in the middle of the room. Several conversations seemed to be in progress and no one took any notice of the self-conscious trio standing in the doorway.

'Help yourself to some coffee,' said Nick, and he left them to go over to a vacant chair on the other side of the room, leaving them feeling horribly conspicuous yet oddly unnoticed. After a moment's hesitation they did as Nick suggested and found places to sit.

'I think we ought to start,' said a woman cutting across the hubbub of voices. 'I see we have three newcomers with us today. Would you like to introduce yourselves?' The conversation died away and eyes were turned towards them. They felt very nervous.

'My name's Ian. I'm a social work student. I'm going to be doing a six-month placement.'

'My name's Sue. I'm a student nurse. I'm here for six weeks.'

'My name's Barbara. I'm applying for a job and I've come to spend a day here.'

'Is that the nursing assistant's job?' someone checked.

And that, to their relief, was that. No more questions. The rest of the meeting was taken up with a discussion about what had happened the night before, in particular about Tony, who had got drunk at a pub, come back to the community and broken a window. It appeared that Nick and the woman who had introduced them were important people here, but it was unclear exactly what were their positions. Some people said nothing during this meeting. One or two looked very morose and Barbara wondered if they were patients. Most were dressed in casual clothes – jeans seemed to be the rule. This surprised Sue, who had expected the staff to wear uniforms.

They were puzzled by some of the words they heard used repeatedly, phrases like 'acting out', 'projecting', 'group dynamics'. They had the uncomfortable feeling that people who were not present were being criticized without the opportunity to defend themselves, which seemed unfair. It emerged from what was said that Tony had become fond of one of the female staff members and had got drunk after she had refused to go out with him. Some of the staff said that this meant he was 'acting out' instead of talking about his feelings in a group. Sue thought it was quite understandable not to want to talk about such personal matters in a group. Barbara wondered why the girl in question had refused Tony's invitation. Ian noticed that the girl herself was saying nothing, just staring into space.

Just before 9 o'clock the meeting ended and everyone got up to leave. The three newcomers stood up too, but with no idea where to go. They suddenly felt lost and awkward again. Nick came up and spoke to them.

'There's a community meeting now followed by a staff feedback meeting at 10. You'll probably find it a bit confusing to begin with, not knowing who's who. After the feedback there are various activity groups – you can decide which one you want to join. This afternoon you'll each be allocated to one of the therapy groups, and there should be some time after that for any questions you might have. Oh, you'll probably be asked to introduce yourselves in the community meeting. We'd better go or we'll be late.'

This information was reassuring but it left many questions. Who was in charge? What was the purpose of the meeting they had just been in, and the one they were going to? Did everyone sit in meetings the whole day? Didn't anyone ever get a chance to talk to anyone on their own?

They entered a large room furnished only with an assortment of soft and hard chairs along each wall. The middle of the room was a large empty space. People were ambling in and taking their seats. Many of the staff were sitting at one end of the room. The residents, or 'members', were dressed like the staff, in jeans and other casual clothes. Apart from recognizing faces there was no way to be sure who was a resident and who was a staff member. The number of men and women was about equal, and most of the residents looked in their twenties or early thirties. There were over thirty people in the room.

The sheer size of the meeting seemed overwhelming, especially to Sue and Barbara, who had never been in anything like this before. Barbara concentrated on how she could make herself as inconspicuous as possible. In marked contrast to the last meeting there was little conversation. People entered and sat in silence. Some held cups of tea or coffee, most just sat, waiting.

'I suppose we ought to start,' said a young man hesitantly.

They had not seen him before, so they assumed he must be a resident. He began by reading out a report about events in the community during the previous day and night. Various names were mentioned. At one point the report said that a resident had been late for his work group. This was interrupted by a gruff voice from somewhere in the room.

'I had a good reason for being late. I was waiting for my probation officer, but he never showed up.'

'Let Roger finish reading the report,' said someone.

'Well, I'm always getting picked on in the reports, they're a load of rubbish.'

'I'm only reading what's written here,' said Roger.

'Arthur always complains,' said a girl. 'At least he gets written about. No one ever mentions me.'

'I'd like to hear the rest of the report,' said one of the staff. Roger continued reading. When he had finished, someone asked where were Tony and one or two other absentees. It was a pity, she said, that Tony had not been here to listen to what had been read out about him. Nick then told the meeting about his conversation with Tony earlier that morning, and said it seemed as though Tony was set on getting himself kicked out of the community. Nick suggested that a member of Tony's small group might be able to persuade him to come to the meeting. One of the residents said he would try, and left the room.

'I think the chairman has forgotten that we have some newcomers with us today,' said a voice from somewhere. Sue, Ian and Barbara felt the spotlight turned on them. Barbara felt panicky as the other two introduced themselves, but heard herself do the same in a sort of disembodied voice. No one asked them any questions after they had introduced themselves. In fact, quite the opposite, a deep silence seemed to descend on the meeting, so suddenly that it might almost have been at a signal. Was it something I said? thought Barbara, who had spoken last. She wasn't sure what she had said, such had been her state of nervousness.

They've just noticed us, thought Ian, and they don't want us here. Perhaps they are going to ask us to leave.

Sue was feeling quite detached from it all. She thought it was rather amusing, all those people waiting for something to happen. If they don't have anything more to discuss why don't they end the meeting, she wondered, but repressed an urge to smile – someone might ask her what was funny and she could not possibly tell them. The silence continued.

'I feel pretty awkward in this silence,' came a voice from somewhere, 'and I think if I were one of the new arrivals I'd feel even more awkward. It seems we don't really want to welcome them.'

Oh God, not the spotlight again, thought Barbara, feeling a bit sick.

'I do feel apprehensive at the moment,' said Ian, glad of the opportunity to speak. Barbara could not believe how brave he was. Sue was debating whether to ask what the meeting was for when the resident who had gone out to fetch Tony returned. Tony could not be found, and a discussion immediately began about whether more people should go out to look for him. Some were in favour of this but others thought it would only encourage Tony to carry on acting in this way. No agreement could be reached since everyone seemed to have a different view. Instead of concentrating on coming to a decision, the newcomers were puzzled when some of the staff began to comment on other things. There was a remark that Tony was not the only member of the community who wanted to have a special relationship with one of the staff, and that some people were using the present situation to avoid talking about their feelings towards other people in the room. This struck the trio as a confusing diversion from the task in hand – deciding what to do about Tony – and they had the impression that no one was really in control of the meeting. This impression was confirmed when Arthur repeated his opinion that it was all a load of rubbish and got up and walked out of the room. As he did so Tony appeared. Someone said it was starting to become like a railway station. Everyone laughed and the tension in the room eased.

'I'm glad you decided to come after all.'

'I wanted to know what people were saying about me.'

The meeting fell into silence again, but not for long.

'I feel pretty pissed off with the way you've been behaving, Tony. You treat this place like a doss-house,' said a resident.

'Why should I care what anyone else feels? No one cares how I feel.'

'That's not true,' said a girl. 'Sarah cares, or you wouldn't have asked her out.'

'That stupid cow.'

Sarah, who had hardly taken part till now, bit her lip and seemed near to tears.

'If I was Sarah I'd brain you for saying that,' said the girl.

'I think Sarah can speak for herself,' said Nick.

'I'm sorry,' said Sarah, 'I feel quite upset over all this.' Tears began to roll down her cheeks. The newcomers were disturbed to see a staff member showing such emotion in front of the residents. Sue wondered if Sarah would get into trouble for becoming over-involved, as one of the nurses at her hospital had done.

'I think,' said Nick, 'that it's good Tony should see that people do care, and that he can upset them when he acts the way he does.'

'I thought I could help Tony better by talking on our own,' said Sarah. 'He said he couldn't talk in the groups. When he started telling me lots of things in confidence I found it very difficult, I didn't know what to do. I wanted to bring it up in the group, but Tony said he would leave the community if I did that.' She stopped, seemingly at a loss for words.

'I think it's really good that you've been able to bring this into the community meeting,' said one of the staff. Other people nodded sympathetically, and some then spoke of their own difficulties when relationships in the community created divided loyalties between individuals and the community. The atmosphere in the meeting gradually changed from one of tension and confrontation to one of sharing feelings and problems.

The newcomers were surprised at how quickly the time had passed when the chairman announced that it was time to end the meeting. They were still puzzled at the lack of decisions or answers in the meeting. No one had said what the rule was about passing on information from a private conversation, or about how far personal relationships were allowed to go. Tony had still been reluctant to talk openly about his feelings towards Sarah, and Arthur had not returned to the meeting. When the meeting ended nothing had been resolved, yet the newcomers felt that they knew a lot more about the community and its members than they had done an hour ago. They were beginning to feel involved and interested, although as yet more like spectators at a play than members of the community. The staff gradually left the room. No one indicated where they should go and they followed along behind, hoping they were going in the right direction.

If they expected the staff meeting which followed to answer their questions they were disappointed, but at least the events in the community began to fall into some perspective. The 'feedback', as this meeting was called, was dominated by three or four of the staff who discussed and even argued about what this or that had 'meant', and about what had been 'going on' in the community in recent weeks. One said that the community was being split by special staff–resident relationships which were not 'fed back' to the community. Another said that the staff were not expressing their differences and 'acting out'; a third thought that it was the residents who were trying to split the staff. Surprisingly, someone said that the meeting had shown that the community was functioning well.

They were grateful when one of the silent people said that she felt confused by all the different points of view. Someone else said that there seemed to be a lot of competitiveness between a few of the staff, who discussed things in a way that made it difficult for others to join in.

'I wonder how the newcomers are feeling,' said Nick.

'I felt involved in the community meeting,' said Ian, 'but I still feel unclear about what the rules are about staff and residents.'

One or two staff nodded in agreement.

'What I wanted to ask,' said Sue, 'is what the purpose of the meetings is. It seems everyone discusses things but nothing gets decided.'

There was a pause.

'How about you?' someone asked. Barbara was dreading this, she had nothing sensible to say.

'I don't really know how I feel at the moment. There's so much to take in.'

To her surprise some of the staff nodded sympathetically. Then someone asked who would be free to see so-and-so's relatives if they came up today and the conversation changed course again. The newcomers were left feeling that no clear guidance or answers to their questions had been given. It was a feeling they were to become familiar with.

Following the staff feedback meeting everyone went off to join different activities. Sue joined the kitchen group which was preparing lunch for the community. After the uncertainties and elusiveness of the meetings it was a very welcome change to be engaged in a down-to-earth, practical job, with an opportunity to talk to people one at a time. Barbara joined the art group. Large sheets of paper were rolled out on the floor and everyone took part in creating a large painting with the simple instruction from the art therapist to paint whatever they felt like painting. In half an hour they had produced a huge, riotously coloured network of flowers, faces, trees, squiggles, loops and roads, and then sat around it talking about what it looked like and how they had felt while doing it. Ian joined the cleaning group and was given the job of picking up and tidying all the magazines. Other members of his group were brushing the stairs and tidying the communal rooms. A 'domestic' member of staff was vacuum-cleaning the carpets because safety regulations did not permit residents to use electrical appliances – a source of continuing conflict between the community and its parent organization, a resident told Ian.

At 12 o'clock they all had lunch with the residents. Some of the staff also ate with the residents while others went off to the canteen of the main hospital. It was noticeable that one or two residents seemed eager to ask them questions while others ignored them. They were asked why they had come, what they were studying and what they thought of the community. They learned that most residents had been there between three and twelve months, and that while some liked it others were unhappy and talked of leaving. One or two of the dissatisfied residents seemed to take the opportunity to unburden themselves to the newcomers, telling them of the strict rules, the boredom, the feeling that they weren't getting anywhere. One girl asked Barbara if she knew of any other therapeutic community she could go to, but Barbara didn't know.

After lunch they each joined one of the small groups. These met on three afternoons a week for an hour and a half. Each group had seven or eight residents and two staff members. They sat round in a circle. Here again, as in the morning community meeting, they felt rather like intruders. More so in a way, because more intimate and personal things were talked about. Residents spoke about their feelings towards one another, and about things that had happened to them outside. There were also quite long silences which seemed more relaxed than in the large morning meeting. They noticed that the staff sometimes took the lead in steering the discussion, asking questions or bringing in silent members, and sometimes sat back and let the residents run the group. Ian, who had read about therapeutic communities, was surprised that the staff did not say much about their own feelings or experience.

After the groups had finished the residents went to have tea and the staff stayed behind to talk briefly about what had happened in the group. Then it was time for the promised question and answer session – complete with a welcome pot of tea. They were back in the room they had started in at 8.30 – the green room. That seemed a very long time ago. One, two, three, four, five, six meetings ago, counted Ian. They began to realize how tired they felt. It had been an exhausting day although they had spent most of it sitting down. They were joined by Nick and Sarah, and by Roger, the resident chairman in the community meeting. Nick told them that Jean (the woman who had started off the first staff meeting) couldn't come and sent her apologies. He had hoped that more staff would have come but it was always difficult to get people to go to things at this time of day – sometimes they just wanted to unwind.

'I'm not surprised,' said Sue, 'I'm exhausted.'

'Do you mean the staff feel the same way as the residents do?' asked Ian.

'How do you mean?' asked Nick.

'Some of the residents were saying at lunch time and in the small group that they didn't like being here or having to go to all the group meetings. And there was Tony this morning.'

'Yes, well I suppose we all feel that way from time to time. It's not an easy place to work.'

'What I wanted to ask,' said Sue, 'was why none of the staff introduced themselves when we were asked to. I still don't know who anyone is or what anyone does.

Nick nodded slowly.

'Yes, I suppose it's difficult to know where to begin. I mean, everybody introducing themselves, you wouldn't have remembered.'

'What do you do?' Ian asked directly.

'Well, my title is "charge nurse" but that doesn't really tell you what I do. I mean I don't go around giving people pills and injections.'

'What is your role then?'

'Basically it involves being a member of the community, taking part in meetings, doing things with residents like cleaning dishes and playing table tennis, then at other times standing back and trying to understand what's going on, like why somebody walks out of a meeting or gets upset over something. Sometimes I act as a facilitator – in my small group – helping residents talk about their feelings. But often other residents are better at doing that than I am. I think an important part of my job is being around as a support, for staff as well as residents.'

'What roles do other staff take?' asked Barbara.

'There isn't a clear distinction between the roles different staff take while we're in the community. Although we each have different professional backgrounds a lot depends on the personal experience of the individuals.'

'But there must be some hierarchy,' said Sue. 'After all, it is a hospital.'

'Yes, but not the kind of hospital you're used to,' replied Nick, a bit sharply Sue thought. 'Here the hierarchy is a lot flatter. People don't tell others what to do, decisions are discussed by everyone who's affected. I trained in a general hospital and I can tell you it's a lot different.'

'But at the end of the day isn't it the doctors who are in charge?'

'There may be times when one of the doctors takes the lead, but there are other times when I or one of the other staff take the lead. There isn't just one leader.'

'I know everyone is supposed to be equal and all that,' said Ian, 'but I get the feeling that there are some hidden rules that no one admits to.'

'How do you mean?'

'Well, for example, it seemed to me that only certain staff were allowed to give their views in the staff meeting, and that staff came to the rescue of another staff member in the community meeting.'

'You mean Sarah this morning?' asked Nick.

'I think it can seem like that.' Sarah spoke for the first time. 'I remember feeling the same way when I first arrived, three months ago. No one would explain anything, you just had to work it out for yourself.'

'Wouldn't it be possible to give everyone a handout when they came,' asked Sue, 'explaining how the unit works?'

'We do that – there's a new one being worked on at the moment by some of the residents,' answered Nick.

'But people still feel the same way,' added Roger.

'I didn't mind about not knowing people's names,' said Barbara, 'but I thought some of the groups were really difficult to take part in. I found it easier to talk to people over lunch and in the art session this morning.'

'I still don't know what the purpose of the meetings is,' added Sue. 'If the aim is to get residents to talk about their problems, surely it would be better if they met a staff member individually. I don't think I would want to talk about my problems in front of a whole lot of people.'

'Why not?' asked Nick.

'I'd want to choose who I talked to.'

'I know what you mean,' said Roger. 'When I first came here I was terrified of the large groups – afraid to fidget or cough or do anything to attract attention. It wasn't much better in the small groups – there were only two or three people in the community I felt I trusted, and none of them were in my group. I felt that if I said anything they'd use it against me. It took a long time before I began to feel that I was one of the community, that people actually cared about me.'

'How did that change happen?' asked Barbara.

'I think it was when I wasn't the newest member any more, you know, the baby. When other people came and I saw them feeling the way I had, then I thought, well I'm part of this community, I can help them.'

'Yes, I think I feel that talking to you,' Sarah said to the newcomers. 'I remember feeling that I couldn't say anything in the meetings. I still feel that sometimes.'

'How did you feel being the centre of attention in the community meeting?' asked Ian. 'I mean, I sort of wondered if you were putting it on for effect.'

'Oh, I don't agree,' said Barbara. 'I thought it must have been really hard for her.'

'Well,' said Ian, 'it seemed such a good demonstration, you know, "This is how a therapeutic community works".'

'That's like your feelings that there are hidden rules, some behind-the-scenes manipulation,' said Nick.

Ian nodded, but felt uncomfortable having what he said commented on in this way.

'It took me a long time to pluck up the courage to say something,' said Sarah, 'but when I did it wasn't so bad. I think when you first come you're terribly afraid of saying the wrong thing, but after a while you begin to realize that there isn't really a right or wrong thing, and you just have to be yourself.'

'That's what worried me,' said Barbara. 'In the small group this afternoon, I kept trying to think of something to say, but by the time I could think of something people were talking about something different. So in the end, I didn't say anything.'

'I felt more like an observer,' said Sue, 'so it was all right to sit back and not say anything. I think that might change, if I get to know the residents a bit more.'

'Yes,' said Barbara, 'there was a feeling that the staff had it all worked out and if you said anything you might upset what they were trying to do.'

'It seems you all had a similar feeling,' said Nick, 'of being outsiders, not sure how to fit in or what part to play.'

They all nodded in agreement. Ian was feeling annoyed. He felt that they, in particular he himself, were being analysed by Nick. It's all very well for you, he thought, sitting back and watching us grope around and make fools of ourselves. But he couldn't actually say this. What he did say was, 'Do any of the staff leave because they feel they don't fit in?'

It was Sarah who answered. 'Someone left about a month ago. She was the next staff member to arrive after me. She was very spontaneous and I think she felt too restricted by all the meetings and the daily structure.'

'Don't you feel restricted?' Ian asked.

'Yes, I do, sometimes. But I think it's more to do with my wanting someone to tell me what to do, being afraid to stick my neck out in case I get laughed at or criticized.'

Barbara felt both sympathetic and impressed listening to Sarah. It was just what she often felt, not only today but in lots of situations, but she wouldn't have been able to put it into words that clearly.

There was a pause. Nick looked at his watch. He said he had another meeting to go to and they probably wanted to get away and mull over their impressions of the day. Barbara would be contacted as soon as the staff had had a chance to discuss her application. There would be another, more formal, interview. And with that the meeting, and their first day, were over.

Travelling home, each was conscious of an element of surprise in what they had experienced. Sue had not looked forward to coming to Alexander House – doing psychiatry had seemed a bit of a chore. She would have been content to observe things passively and wait for the time to pass. Instead she had been surprised at how interesting she had found it. Admittedly some of the staff seemed rather strange, with their peculiar jargon and search for hidden meanings in ordinary things. But what people talked about – what residents talked about – seemed much more real than she had anticipated from reading books and going to lectures on psychiatry. They got upset over the sorts of things that would upset her, like being ignored or made to do things they didn't want to. The atmosphere was a lot more open than on general hospital wards – a student who cried in front of patients would probably be

sent home or transferred to another ward – and the staff were able to disagree with each other in a way that she had never seen before. Ian might be
right about things going on 'behind the scenes', but you wouldn't expect to
know everything on your first day.

Ian was experiencing a rather different state of surprise. He had expected
the day to be enjoyable and stimulating, but now he found himself feeling
confused and annoyed. The staff were not as spontaneous as they pretended
they were. The things they said sounded rather 'pat' and automatic and Nick
had been evasive in his answers, ending the meeting to avoid being challenged. Obviously he, Ian, was too perceptive for the staff's liking. Rather
than risk having more questions turned back on him he decided that for the
rest of the week he wouldn't say anything, just stay quiet and observe as Sue
had done.

Barbara had expected a therapeutic community to be a friendly, informal
place, with little distinction between staff and residents, everyone taking
part in an equal way. She had been surprised at the amount of organization
and formality. Different groups at different times for different purposes, different people taking different roles – it all seemed artificial. The natural,
easygoing interactions she had imagined did occur, but only in the art group
and at lunch time. She had begun to feel during the day that it was quite beyond her to understand, let alone play a useful part in all these activities.
Then hearing Sarah talking gave her hope; the staff were not all so different
from her, in time she might also be able to express herself like that. Perhaps
they wouldn't offer her the job anyway. But if they did – would she take it? It
gave her butterflies inside to think about that.

CHAPTER 11

Staff Roles and Some Dos and Don'ts for Beginners

STAFF ROLES

The roles of staff members in a therapeutic community can be described under a number of headings. What follows is a practical rather than theoretical list. The kind of knowledge and awareness needed to undertake these roles is addressed in the next chapter.

Participating Oneself as a Member of the Community

In traditional health settings all sickness is located in the patient and all health in the staff. The patient is not encouraged to show his or her healthy, effective capacities and the staff member is not free to show vulnerability or inadequacy. In a therapeutic community this oversimplified stereotyping is partly tackled by staff and residents sharing in everyday tasks. For example, staff will take their turn on domestic rotas or other practical tasks, while residents will be able to take responsibility showing visitors round and explaining to them how the community works.

In addition to this general equalization of status, a staff member may work closely with a patient helping her to carry out tasks that have both practical and emotional importance, such as organizing and providing food for the community (Irwin 1995). As well as overcoming the split between the patient in the 'sick' role and staff member in the 'know-it-all' role, this also provides a supportive, calming presence while the patient struggles with new challenges.

With staff and residents working closely alongside each other there is always a potential risk that the therapeutic purpose of this sharing and intimacy will be forgotten or put under pressure by the personal needs of the staff member or the desire of the resident to avoid the difficult issues. The previous chapter showed how this could happen, especially for a relatively new staff member. If relationships within the community are to be therapeutic, and the short-term comforts of exclusive pairings resisted, the therapeutic purpose of relationships must be supported by the culture and expectations of the therapeutic community, with regular staff meetings to review roles and relationships. This emphasizes the need for training, supervision and staff support in therapeutic communities, where everyday relationships are the 'bread and butter' of the therapeutic work.

Preserving the Boundaries Needed for the Community to be Therapeutic

Boundaries include the time, place and purpose of different activities, and where responsibility lies for different decisions. A clear structure is especially important for people with little control over their impulses. The routine of activities being set in a predictable time framework provides an external structure of containment which the patient can gradually internalize. Feelings can be better managed because there is a known time and place and relationship where they can be expressed.

Since Rapoport's original research at the Henderson (Rapoport 1960), it has been a common finding that therapeutic communities can go through oscillations in which there are periods when the whole community functions well – the structures are observed, senior residents support newer ones, responsibilities can be fully shared between staff and residents – followed by periods of more disturbed and potentially destructive behaviour, often after the more experienced and successful patients have left. At these times it is the staff who must take the lead to re-establish the structure and norms of the community until the residents are ready and able to take responsibility again. The amount of boundary maintenance required from staff is therefore likely to vary according to the current state of the community.

Modelling (Demonstrating by Example) Desired Behaviour

One of the main ways to maintain boundaries is for staff members to demonstrate their own commitment to them. Understanding the patient's actions in relation to any boundaries requires the boundaries themselves to be clear. If staff do not keep to the boundaries the risk is that the boundaries soon disappear or become vague and indistinct. When a therapeutic community is functioning well – at a constructive stage of the cycle – the more experienced patients or residents will also act as role models for newer members, and benefit from doing so. But modelling is not just about boundaries. Staff (and senior residents) can also model openness and honesty and risk taking. If a member of staff is willing to try something he or she is not sure of – a competition, a sport, having to entertain by singing or telling a joke – what is modelled is a nondefensive approach to uncertainty, a willingness to experiment, to risk looking foolish. If staff can take the risk it makes it easier for residents to have a go.

Provision of Learning Experiences

Within a therapeutic community there is a wide range of tasks available both for individual members and for groups. These can include practical domestic tasks such as buying and cooking food, organizing activities, running meetings, taking part in decisions affecting the community, introducing visitors and new residents, contributing to one another's therapy. An important part of the staff members' role is being able to judge when to take the lead and when to stand back. The goal is always to try to facilitate a useful learning experience. Getting something wrong, like buying the wrong food or letting a meeting go off course, is a useful learning experience if it is followed by feedback, discussion, understanding, and a chance to try again. Standing back is not be equated with abdication from professional responsibility, but a thoughtful provision of learning experiences. Short-term inefficiency in task performance is accepted for longer-term gains. It is of interest that the underlying principle here is quite compatible with skills-teaching models, but with the added element of using peer feedback and exploring the emotional significance of things going wrong.

Using Therapeutic Interventions in Groups

The skills of being able to intervene therapeutically in groups are relevant in therapeutic communities, and the therapeutic factors identified by Yalom (1985) apply just as much to groups in therapeutic communities as in outpatient settings. Whiteley and Collis (1987) found that three of these factors were particularly prominent in their study of patients in the Henderson: learning from interpersonal actions, acceptance (especially in the early stages of treatment) and self-understanding. Many approaches to group work can be used to encourage the emergence of these factors by building a climate of trust and openness between group members, including group analysis, art therapy, psychodrama, transactional analysis. However, there are some 'techniques' that tend to impair the emergence of group therapeutic factors, such as emotionally detached questions, confrontation without subsequent support, or making aloof interpretations. Tom Main (1975) described how, particularly in large groups of thirty or more, the sense of depletion and anonymity can be so strong that each person feels that only 'Nobel Prize winning thoughts' are acceptable. In such a climate an expression of someone's thoughts in ordinary, everyday language can bring relief from this fantasy and enable people to recover their capacity to think and speak.

Encouraging Exploration of the Meaning of Behaviour

Having made the point above, it still remains a core task of the therapeutic community to help patients to recognize and understand the emotional difficulties which tasks, responsibilities and relationships within the community bring to the fore. Often these will involve the repetition of the same difficulties that have occured before in the patient's life. A staff member may offer an interpretation of the meaning of these difficulties to the patient, making the connection between the past and the present, but often it will be more effective when patients do this for each other, using their own experiences to offer interpretations to a fellow patient of why they found a particular situation difficult to cope with.

Attending to the Dynamics of the Community, in Particular where Processes Destructive of the Community as a Learning Environment May Arise

Such processes include scapegoating, splitting and idealization. For example, a common weakness in a therapeutic community is that the members idealize the community and see any criticism from outside as the product either of ignorance or of envy. This insularity creates two risks. First that internal criticism or doubts within the community are suppressed, cohesiveness becomes a kind of tyranny, and the culture of enquiry so central to maintaining a learning environment is lost. The second risk is that real threats from outside the community are not dealt with, leading to loss of the external support necessary to the community's survival. It is noteworthy that successful, long-lived communities have always become adept at developing good relationships with both the wider professional community and the local neighbourhood.

Attending to One's Own Emotional Involvement

Working in a therapeutic community is probably one of the most emotionally challenging jobs imaginable. There is no uniform or desk to hide behind. Everything is potentially exposed. The staff member must be open to understanding his or her own emotional involvement in, and contribution to, the dynamics of relationships within the community, and able to use the opportunities in staff groups, external training and personal therapy to examine these. Genuineness is the only workable strategy (see dos and don'ts below) but the risks of over-involvement and burn-out are high and staff must also learn to balance their work involvement with non-work activities – an issue addressed in more detail by Meinrath and Roberts (1982).

Being Able to Describe and Explain the Community

To be able to explain the therapeutic community model – its purpose and how it works – to newcomers, visitors and outsiders is important for the reasons mentioned earlier. The success of a therapeutic community may depend partly on patients' relatives, referrers, and service purchasers having a good appreciation of why it works as it does. Having a clear idea of how it works will also help to maintain staff morale when the pressures are stressful, as in the imaginary scenario described in the last chapter. And a coincidental value of having to explain something to others is that it helps one's own understanding – as anyone who has had to prepare a teaching session on a subject knows.

SOME DOS AND DON'TS FOR BEGINNERS

If, like the characters in the previous chapter, you find yourself visiting or joining a therapeutic community for the first time – or perhaps a similar kind of unit – then in addition to the list of staff roles just given it may be useful to have a few dos and don'ts as a general guide in the first weeks. These weeks will almost certainly be difficult ones, as you try to find or create a place for yourself that suits both you and the community. This process may be eased if you bear in mind the following points.

Do look on this as an opportunity to learn about yourself as well as others

Whatever your professional reason for entering a therapeutic community it will also have a tremendous personal impact. Be prepared for this and take it as an opportunity to learn about your own feelings and responses, as well as about other people and their problems.

Don't expect to be told exactly what to do

If you are a student or trainee you may be used to receiving instructions about what you are expected to do. In a therapeutic community you are more likely to be given a brief welcome and left to get on with things and find your own personal place, so –

Do talk to people

Introduce yourself, let people know who you are and why you have come. There is no hierarchy of the type where those at the bottom must only speak if they are spoken to so you need not worry about speaking out of turn. (In concept-based therapeutic communities there are certain formalities about relations between residents at different levels in the hierarchy.) At first you may not always know if the person you are speaking to is a resident or staff member, or what seniority they have in the community. This doesn't matter – get to know people as individuals. You will soon start to know who is who in the community by the roles they take in the various activities and meetings.

Do get involved in what is going on

Take whatever opportunities present themselves for taking part in the life of the community. These may include jobs like cleaning and tidying, preparing food, sharing meals with residents, taking part in games and recreational activities, simply talking to people, and participating in the various group meetings.

Do be yourself

In a therapeutic community it is all right to be as you are – shy or outgoing, easy going or critical, tense or relaxed. Don't feel you have to pretend to be someone else, different from the way you are when you are not at work.

Do say what you actually feel

By saying what you really think and feel you will let the other members of the community get to know you and you will start to feel part of the community. If you hold back from saying what you feel you are likely to remain feeling on the 'outside'.

Don't hold back for fear of saying the wrong thing

Newcomers often worry about saying the wrong thing and upsetting someone. People do get upset or angry at times, but learning to cope with such feelings is one of the aims of a therapeutic community so there is no need to prevent this from happening. Sometimes this means letting other people express their feelings even if it makes you feel bad or guilty. And the other staff or residents will be able to support someone who is upset so you need not feel 'on your own'. Newcomers also often assume that the staff have carefully laid plans for running meetings which the beginner might accidentally muck up. In practice there are seldom plans that are as specific as the newcomer imagines. Indeed, if there were such plans worked out in advance by some of the staff, then the community would fail in its aim of getting every member – including you – to share in the responsibility for what goes on in the community.

Don't feel you have to produce 'pearls of wisdom'

Ordinary, everyday statements can be as helpful as clever interpretations or wise advice. In group meetings, especially large ones, it is easy to imagine that because so many people are listening anything you say must sound brilliant. In practice such efforts often reduce participation and make the atmosphere more tense. Ordinary expressions of interest or personal experience tend to make it more comfortable and intimate. Your own experience of hearing other people talk will confirm this.

Don't be put off if you don't get an answer

It can be unnerving when you say something in a meeting and no one responds, or someone changes the subject. All sort of thoughts crowd in: I've said the wrong thing; they disapprove; they don't care. Actually, you have been heard, but in a group which follows a process of free discussion, themes get taken up and dropped according to the current preoccupations of the group members. It's not like an ordinary conversation (although these may occur). What one person says may get taken up straight away by someone else, may be returned to later, or may be taken away and thought about by someone.

It can also be frustrating when you make what you think is a useful suggestion only to be told it wouldn't work, it has already been tried, or that you don't understand things yet. It may seem that these responses are simply defending the status quo, that the staff are unwilling to listen to new ideas. This may be true, but maybe a newcomer is reacting to his or her own experience of becoming a member of the community. This needs to be worked out – with others if necessary.

A final do – do take things as they come

You will probably get most out of the first few weeks of starting to work in a therapeutic community if you are not in a rush to establish a therapeutic role for yourself or to understand the reason behind everything. Allow yourself to experience what it is like not to know, what it is like being new, getting to know the people, voicing your own first impressions and listening to other people's, participating in activities and being yourself. What at first seemed to be a frustrating lack of structure and guidance will become a rewarding opportunity to learn in a very direct way about personal relationships, healthy and disturbed, and the ways in which they can be understood and changed.

CHAPTER 12

Questions of Training

Jeff Roberts

In the first edition of this book we said:

> The question of what sort of training is generally appropriate for therapeutic community staff has barely begun to be asked, let alone answered.

The question is now being asked but the answer has not been agreed upon. Various suggestions have been made as to the form which training could take, but it seems at present that it will be some years before any kind of nationally recognized scheme is established.

As a result of recent developments, which include the intended establishment of two further Henderson-type communities in Birmingham and Manchester and a proposed doubling of therapeutic community places in the prison service, it seems probable that there will be an increasing demand for therapeutic communities over the next ten years. At the moment there are scarcely enough skilled and trained staff to look after therapeutic communities safely. Where will the staff and senior therapists for new therapeutic communities come from?

The environment surrounding therapeutic communities has changed considerably in the fifteen years since we first gave our attention to therapeutic community training in this chapter. It now contains the results of governance by a prime minister (Margaret Thatcher) who publicly denied the existence of society. The group and community have both, to a degree, lost status and credibility, whilst the individual has been promoted to a level which denies his/her dependence on group-based structures.

There has been a concurrent paradoxical development. This is the pursuit of a long-term government policy of replacing 'institutional care' with 'care in the community'. This massive project involves a progressive transfer of the care of vulnerable individuals from institutions back to the community. It is a policy which depends on a society made up of communities for its success.

In many ways this policy has been a success. There are now far fewer people in long-term institutional care, and hospital admissions for psychiatric illness are measured in weeks rather than months. The untoward social effects of this policy have been well documented (Leff 1997). In this chapter I need only consider it as it relates to therapeutic communities and therapeutic community training.

The policy has had a significant detrimental effect on therapeutic community provision within the National Health Service. As discussed in Chapter 6 it has led to the closure of a number of hospitals in which there were thriving therapeutic communities for the acute and long-term mentally ill. Very brief inpatient admission to a highly disturbed acute ward followed by rapid discharge back to community and family has made therapeutic community provision in our National Health Service not only redundant but also more or less impossible to deliver. However, many mentally ill people recover poorly and require hostels and day units which prove to be most effective when conducted as therapeutic communities. Moreover the rehabilitation wards for the people who have come to be called 'the new long stay' work effectively when conducted as modified therapeutic communities. The work in such communities is demanding of a particular kind of sensitivity and patience. Staff need to be carefully selected and to have focused additional training relevant to this task.

A further development has been the reorganization of health and social service provision. This has had two influences on therapeutic community work. First there is a growing demand for evidence-based efficient and focused practice. Second, the financial structure of the services has been shifted largely to local funding.

The therapeutic community does not deliver rapid results and is usually perceived as too diffuse a method to be granted a place where efficient and focused practice is required. Scientific research into treatment methods has tended to be displaced by audit exercises of little depth. The therapeutic community does not come out well of short-term audit exercises – although it has been argued that it need have nothing to fear from this process (Knowles 1992) – and needs professionally designed and sophisticated research.

The local funding shift has been very destructive. Many therapeutic communities are specialist services covering a large catchment area. The Henderson Hospital, for instance, has long been a national resource. Local funding, which has been linked to recurrent rounds of budget cuts, has left the Henderson and other therapeutic communities vulnerable to money-saving exercises. As a result, the life of many therapeutic communities during the past twenty years has been skewed in the direction of marketing and self-justification. There is a round of cuts every year and a therapeutic community once targeted often has to save itself as an annual event.

Internationally we have seen significant flux in therapeutic emphasis. Our cousins over the Atlantic have taken to psychopharmacology with a typical sceptical enthusiasm. I would suggest that the United States is unique in being able to supply diehard medical psychopharmacologists who are also trained in psychoanalysis. The Netherlands, once a therapeutic community stronghold, has given way to medicalization. Made of wood after all? Italy, having abolished institutional care, is now realizing that something is required in its place and is developing an interesting new therapeutic community culture. Finally, in the former Soviet Union there is an enthusiastic embracing of Western methods and thinking. Democratic methods of treatment have a lot to offer here but need dedicated and persistent teachers.

We are also witness to a growing demand that psychotherapists and counsellors are accredited. This ensures quality control and that the client can anticipate delivery of treatment by a practitioner who is well enough trained and does what he/she says he does. In the long run this means that only those therapies which maintain standards and integrity over time will survive. The therapeutic community method will need to demonstrate that it is an effective treatment method and that it has practitioners capable of delivering in a predictable professional way. Likewise, a therapeutic community may be required to be accredited as an organization which provides a therapeutic environment and process which comes up to agreed standards of 'quality and quantity'.

There will be a need to accredit: training courses, individual graduates of courses and also therapeutic communities themselves. The final category is necessary in order to ensure that a specific therapeutic community is a suitable context for treatment and also for training.

It seems to me that therapeutic community training will be essential for all who plan a long-term career in therapeutic community work. However, there is still a great deal of uncertainty about this and the individual therapeutic community staff member has a great deal of freedom to decide on how he or she may develop. The current trend is for the ambitious therapeutic community staff member to collect a portfolio of skills, experience, qualifications, courses and degrees. This represents his or her non-accreditable therapeutic community training. In the next few years, this will, I believe, need to give way to a clear cut pathway to an accreditable training for therapeutic community work and at a higher level for therapeutic community 'management'.

Contemporary practice continues to vary widely conditioned by local needs and preferences. There is a range of opportunities and requirements, from therapeutic communities in which no special training or experience is required through to those in which the staff participate in a variety of internal and external training programmes and undertake a personal experience of therapy. Different levels of expectation about training are not surprising, considering the diversity of origins of therapeutic communities.

Therapeutic communities in large psychiatric hospitals and prisons were created in order to improve the outcome of incarceration. As a result, staff morale improved as they began to discover a more challenging job which gave hope to both them and their clients. Those who had become instutionalized in the old system often became very uncomfortable and either left or stayed to sabotage the new therapeutic community. Staff who rose to the challenge began to need and to ask for training.

The small, specialized communities of the democratic, psychoanalytic or group analytic type, such as the Henderson Hospital, Cassel Hospital and Ingrebourne Centre, usually do expect staff to pursue further training. There is rarely a clear indication as to what the best training might be. The most ambitious staff members may seek psychotherapy training. What is rarely acknowledged it that individual psychoanalytic training or individual psychoanalytic therapy training is almost entirely irrelevant for therapeutic community work and group analytic training is only partially relevant.

These communities often provide extensive in-house teaching and even arrange short courses for outsiders. Most communities offer their new staff an organized programme of supervision, seminars and support groups while others expect staff to obtain their training through participation in outside courses. Where an independent organization runs a number of communities, it may, like the Richmond Fellowship, offer a career structure linked to its own organized training programme. Such a training may be respected by other therapeutic communities when employing staff but it is only a partial fulfilment of training needs and is not accreditable.

Training in the hierarchically structured concept-based therapeutic communities is, for ex-addict staff, primarily the experience of going through such a community as a resident. For professional staff, too, participation as a resident may be an important part of training. These communities may have their own career structure which enables them to employ and promote people who have no formal professional training, as is often the case for ex-addict staff.

Those communities – loosely collected under the heading of alternative asylum or anti-psychiatry, such as the Philadelphia Association and Arbours Association – also do extensive in-house training. The Arbours has intensive psychotherapy training for those working with seriously disturbed clients.

Communities for the handicapped often accept people as 'co-workers' who live as permanent members of the community. In other cases the work may be seen as a period of experience 'en route' to more specialized professional or therapeutic work, or as an adjunct to training in psychotherapy.

With such a varied pattern of training options and expectations, you may wonder how to decide about your own training. In this chapter I will try to deal with a number of questions which will concern the person who is either working in a therapeutic community and wishing to increase their skill and understanding, or considering the possibility of doing so and wondering whether qualifications or training would help. I will look at these issues in terms of four questions:

(1)   Do I need a professional qualification or a university degree before going on to train for therapeutic community work?

(2)   If I have a degree or a professional qualification, do I need any further training for therapeutic community work?

(3)   If training for therapeutic community work, what do I need to learn?

(4)   What are the resources for training and learning?

DO I NEED A PROFESSIONAL QUALIFICATION?

Before proceeding with this section I will clarify the differences between professional qualifications and academic achievement. A member of a profession often, but not always, has a university degree. He or she, however, always has had experience and will always have a qualification which has been accredited and is registerable with a professional body such as the General Medical Council or the Royal College of Nursing.

There are a number of routes to working at an increasingly more responsible job in a therapeutic community.

(1)   If you are uncertain about what kind of work you want to do and need real experience of working in a caring environment you might become a care assistant or work as a volunteer. This will give invaluable experience.

(2)   Having decided on the type of work which interests you and for which you have aptitude then professional training can be considered. This type of training is effectively an apprenticeship. It requires a balance between skill acquisition, supervised practice and knowledge acquisition. Eventually you get a qualification, which says you have achieved an adequate standard of safe or ethical practice. The evidence that you have achieved this will be from a mixture of professional examinations and reports of adequate work performance

from the people who have taught or supervised you or for whom you have worked. At this point you can register with a professional body.

(3)   Professional training may be preceded by a university degree course. The degree or higher degree gives evidence of academic achievement not practical skill. A degree is awarded to those who show evidence of having acquired and understood a body of knowledge. The mastery of this body of knowledge is usually classified in an honours degree from pass through to class 1. For academic purposes it would seem that only a 2.I or first class honours degree are worth having. Indeed when I interview people who have taken a degree I tend to look more favourably, other things being equal, on those with a better class of degree. If you have a low-class degree you had best have done something else, like played sport for the university. Otherwise, having a degree will not serve any purpose, unless it is foundation learning for a profession. Even in this case sturdy foundations are advantageous!

There is a new millennium problem which is emerging with an increasing belief in the value of university education. With a growing competitiveness in the job market and a desire for upward mobility and an understandable desire not to undertake tasks perceived as menial (e.g. in nursing, emptying bedpans), there may develop a belief that a 'degree' is worth more than a professional qualification. This may lead to an overemphasis on the academic aspects of a profession so that degrees in nursing and postgraduate degrees in counselling and psychotherapy have been developed which tend to lack a sufficiency of supervised practical work. Project 2000 nurses do far less practical nurse training than those in the much lamented SRN training. Likewise an MA in psychotherapy can have just exactly the wrong emphasis on knowledge and theory skills as opposed to practical skills.

Let us now consider the advantages and disadvantages of professional qualifications and the training that precedes them.

Advantages

There is at present no generally recognized qualification which equips people with core therapeutic community skills and knowledge. This means that someone wanting to work as a staff member might start work as a care assistant (the latter-day equivalent of a social therapist) or volunteer. If a more career-oriented entry is sought then it will be necessary either to qualify first in one of the recognized helping professions, or to work in one of those communities which has its own career structure and system of staff training.

The first advantage of a professional qualification is that it enables you to be employed in an organizational setting on a more permanent basis, and provides a recognized role within an organization. There may be restrictions attached to this role, but there is also greater security of employment. This is important in these times of short-contract employment. It also provides a supportive kinship with those in the same profession, who share the same perspective and interests.

A second advantage is that the qualified professional possesses specific knowledge and skills which can make a special contribution to the therapeutic community. The doctor's knowledge of psychiatric symptoms, the teacher's knowledge of children's developing capacities, the occupational therapist's knowledge of work activities and games can all be valuable resources in a community. Therapeutic communities in many settings are intended to enhance, not replace, individual skills. Even where they offer a distinct alternative to prevailing professional ideas on care and treatment, as in the case of the anti-psychiatry communities, it may be important for someone to be able to make an informed decision – for example, deciding if someone's physical condition requires medical treatment.

Third, and in some ways most important, professional training is good for instilling a sense of the possible, of what can and cannot be achieved, of the limitations of one's skills and knowledge. This is something that therapists without any professional training (and occasionally those with) are prone to ignore. The existence of various therapeutic 'cults' promising a cure for all ills and unhappiness bears witness to a lack of such realism. The trained social worker knows how difficult it is to make the correct decision about whether to leave a child with its potentially violent parents or remove the child to a place of safety. A psychiatrist knows that he cannot read people's minds and is largely reliant on what people are prepared to tell him. In both cases the untrained person sometimes has an unrealistic idea of the possibility of knowing things about other people. Professional training heightens awareness of the limitations of activities which claim to bring about personal or group changes.

Disadvantages

There is a possibility that the trained person may have an unwarranted belief in his superiority over an untrained. This was put forward with some emphasis in the first edition of this book. An anecdote was offered in which a man who has just been awarded a degree fantasizes about the kudos this will earn him in the eyes of the world. I believe there is less naïvety in young people as we approach the millennium. People now know that degrees in themselves are not that helpful in life and, unless they are 1sts or 2.Is, can be a positive hindrance. Unwarranted arrogance is more rapidly crushed. Our naïve young man will now know that he needs professional training in addition to his first degree and that when he finally qualifies this will be after a long and arduous apprenticeship.

People do wish for success and power. It is probably true to say that the most authentic way to get a modicum of these is to work hard to increase one's knowledge and skills. Then one can feel proud – but only if successfully applying the skill and knowledge in co-operation with a group of like-minded colleagues with complementary skills and knowledge. Team skills, indeed, are probably the most important of all. Perhaps those universities who seek talented sportsmen as undergraduates have always known this!

I think the suggestion that a qualification may encourage an unjustified sense of superiority over the less qualified is a relatively minor problem. Certain individuals may go through a phase of this. In most cases they rapidly learn an appropriate humility.

A further problem with a rigorous training leading to a professional qualification is that it may lead to bias towards one's own methods and against ideas and methods involved in other approaches. There can be an almost tribal loyalty. This results in part from a rigidity and narrowness in some trainees and qualified people who have rather specific focused innate skills and interests. More important, such a blinkered form of professional expression results from training of a narrow and rigid kind. An important aspect of a good basic training in a profession is developing an awareness of the interfaces between activities and the overlapping of skills. Each professional training tends to isolate. Little meaningful time in any training is spent developing big pictures of the interrelationship of models and professional skills.

Each new professional turns out inclined to believe that his or her method is the core effective method at least where there is something as uncertain as psychological treatment. The result can be unseemly competition. For many years in our hospitals the medical profession were winning hands down. Then came general management, and now there is a degree of equality, with nurse managers often taking a primary lead. Unfortunately there is a tendency to settle old scores and many doctors don't really understand or believe what has happened.

DO I NEED ANY FURTHER TRAINING?

If you are already qualified in one of the helping professions, or are hoping to be, you may wonder if you need to know anything more to work in a therapeutic community. You may already feel that you know a lot about people and how to help them. If you have chosen to work in a psychotherapeutic field it is likely that you are also aware of a special ability you have, of being able to get closely in touch with the thoughts and feelings of other people. You are keen to get started and, with some justification, feel that you need no further knowledge, particularly in any academic sense. Indeed, with long nights of studying facts and figures and the painful experience of examinations in your recent past, you could have quite an aversion to more learning. Given a few years' experience you expect that the raw materials of talent, enthusiasm and prior training will fit nicely into place, that you will become a good enough staff member. On the other hand, people are increasingly coming round to the idea that to be a good enough staff member (Meinrath and Roberts 1982) in a therapeutic community it is necessary to learn, in an organized way, what therapeutic communities are and how best to participate in them.

There are arguments for both points of view: I have set them out below.

Training is Not Necessary

The therapeutic community ideal embodies egalitarianism. This may imply that given their essential humanity and natural ability anyone can be a therapist without further training. The natural therapeutic abilities of the staff members of a therapeutic community will be elicited by leaders of the staff group and constrained by the formal rules of the organization. Staff members are encouraged to express themselves as freely and honestly as possible and to develop to the full any special talents they may have. At the same time, they are expected to attend community and staff groups regularly, to be responsible and empathic in their confrontations and to avoid developing such relationships with colleagues or clients as will undermine the group ethos or culture. Each staff member may then be expected to produce an optimum performance without further formal training.

The flexibility and enthusiasm of youth is particularly valued. It was with this in mind that Maxwell Jones first introduced 'social therapists' into the Henderson Hospital. These young people, more often women than men, usually in the year before taking up a degree course or other training, would be offered twelve months' work in the therapeutic community. They were (and still are) seen as an important element in the therapeutic functioning of this and other units. Such a process of short-term involvement protects these staff members from becoming stale or over-stressed.

Another reason why training may not be useful is that the therapeutic community approach is not widely applied within the health services. There are therefore only limited career opportunities available for people skilled in therapeutic community work, and the skills required for working in a therapeutic community are not acknowledged in the way health services are organized.

Indeed, if there were a relevant career structure it would need to be cross-disciplinary. Such a structure would be difficult to create in the face of professional rivalries and organizational bureaucracy. At present then, there is nothing tangible to train for, since most people, after a brief period in a therapeutic community, return to a more conventional setting to continue their work. Those who remain in therapeutic communities, working as long-term senior practitioners or leaders of communities, often function quite adequately without having had any formal therapeutic community training.

If there are no special skills required, and most people are encouraged to remain only briefly in the work, it would be pointless to impose on them the rigours of additional training. Having worked hard to achieve a professional qualification, it is reasonable to leave studying behind. You are an expert in a particular field and should be treated as such. You should be able to settle down to enjoy the fruits of earlier labours and not have to expend time, energy and hard-earned money on further training.

Training is Necessary

If the therapeutic community method is to retain or gain status as a recognizable specialist treatment method it will need to be underpinned by a body of knowledge and relevant theory in addition to a requirement for special skills not regularly exercised in other settings. It follows from this that being a therapeutic community worker or manager will require knowledge and theory teaching and skill training. Untrained staff have given and will give the therapeutic community a bad name.

Therapeutic communities are hard to establish and keep going. Some therapeutic communities have short lives and others scarcely get off the ground. On the other hand, mental hospitals and other institutions had comparatively long lives. One of the difficulties in establishing and maintaining therapeutic communities is that they are subject to episodes of destructive behaviour (Roberts 1982). These can be damaging to the organization and may even lead to the closure of the community itself. Such episodes can occur periodically as part of a cycle of oscillation in a community. Training is necessary if staff are to learn to understand and deal with such behaviour, or at least not to participate in it or aggravate it.

In the first edition we said that a further incentive for training was that it would protect the trained person from 'burning out'. This was at a time when 'burn-out' was a rather fashionable idea. This viewpoint has been replaced in the 1990s by 'stress at work'. Employers are now required to evaluate the extent that they are stressing employees and eventually to do something about this. The response often seems to be to offer ten sessions of counselling and to continue imposing the stress.

The outcome of excessive stress at work remains, I believe, burn-out. This term refers to the state of staleness and emotional upset experienced all too often by members of the caring professions, usually relatively early in their career, and which produces disillusionment and defensiveness in the place of enthusiasm and optimism. Two important factors can lead to 'burn-out'. The first is the inevitable and repeated disappointment resulting from clients' progress not coming up to expectations. The second is the way in which members of the helping professions tend to work excessively long hours with too little time and energy devoted to developing their own lives. This is particularly true in therapeutic communities, which provide an exciting career but are not meant to offer their staff members a total way of life.

Burn-out is less of a problem for the short-term staff member, yet it might be argued that the repeated loss of short-term staff, whether through pre-planning or as a result of disillusioned drop-outs, is a waste of talent and partially gathered experience. Indeed, if the short-term staff member makes no attempt to learn from his or her experiences, and is offered no special opportunities to do this, very little may be gained from them. For longer-term 'permanent' staff members, however, the problem of burn-out may threaten both career and well-being. Those who are well informed about therapeutic communities generally and about the expectations attached to their own role in their own community are, I think, less susceptible to burn-out than those who have had no therapeutic community training. There are, of course, people who have worked in therapeutic communities for years and are not burnt-out, or have apparently suffered no ill-effects. Some of these have no doubt devised their own training scheme, while others may be the survivors at the end point of a process of natural selection, although they will probably have gone through many difficult and painful times.

If the avoidance of destructive behaviour, defensive reactions and burn-out appear to be negative reasons for training, the positive side is the potential for a more rewarding career in a therapeutic community. This applies not only in professional terms but in personal ones too. Therapeutic communities have as one of their goals that members should understand the meaning of what is happening to them in their lives and in the therapeutic community itself. Proper training can give people the tools to explore and understand both themselves and therapeutic communities more fully. This will increase the feeling of life in a therapeutic community as an exciting and meaningful unfolding of events rather than a ritualized, incomprehensible and often painful daily grind.

One further argument for training concerns not the individuals who work in them but the survival of therapeutic communities themselves. As described in Chapter 2 the enlightened era of moral treatment disappeared partly because its advocates could not reconcile themselves to the need for professional training. They held the view, advanced in our arguments against training, that personal qualities were all that counted. In the event this meant that communities died when their leaders died or retired. Today a failure to develop appropriate training programmes, associated with a lingering ambivalence over professionalization (Tsegos 1996), may have the same results: communities which are dependent on the skills and dedication of a few enthusiastic individuals. Such communities can survive a long time, but will run into difficulties when the leader leaves or dies. There is also the situation where a therapeutic community enterprise fails to get off the ground. Rather than blame the approach itself, I would argue that such failures often arise through a lack of staff who both believe in and understand the methods they are hoping to put into practice. Enthusiasm allied to skill and understanding is the combination most likely to ensure the continued development of therapeutic communities.

In the present climate of health and social provision another advantage of training is the links it has with quality control and accreditation. One of the best (on the face of it) developments in modern life is quality control linked to the concept of deliverability or otherwise. Quality control can best be achieved when there are mechanisms for ensuring quality of delivery. This can be seen to be happening when a unit is accredited as being a therapeutic community or when staff members can be seen as qualified via an accredited training.

WHAT DO I NEED TO LEARN?

Individual learning is of value to the trainee but is also of value to his/her team, clients, managers and employer.

What should the aim of training be? What kinds of skills and understanding are needed in a therapeutic community? One way to answer this is to discover what people who actually work in therapeutic communities see as their main training needs. David Kennard and I gave a questionnaire to thirty-six staff members from many different communities involved in residential training weekends, entitled 'Learning from Experience in Therapeutic Community Living' (Kennard and Roberts 1978), organized by the British Association of Therapeutic Communities. Prior to coming they were asked what three things they most hoped to gain from the experience. I have summarized the answers below. In the first edition we gave quite elaborate responses to these various requests. In this edition I present them as a wish-list with the intention of provoking thought and giving clearer shape to how training is perceived.

(1)   Knowledge about therapeutic communities and aspects of therapy. (This was the type of learning requested most often.)

(2)   Understanding of the ideas and concepts involved in therapeutic community work.

    (a)   How do they work? What are the different concepts?

    (b)   Where is the place of control for a worker in a therapeutic community?

    (c)   What are the benefits and difficulties of role blurring for staff?

(3)   Increased professional skills and effectiveness.

    (a)   To learn certain techniques which would be of use in dealing with resistant subjects.

    (b)   To balance activity against pure rushing about.

    (c)   To become more sensitive to the group process.

(4)   To learn about myself.

(5)   The experience of being on the other side of being in the role of the patient, resident or client.

(6)   Another experience that therapeutic community staff seek is 'being able to meet and talk with people who work in other communities'.

This is a 'consumer' list, but I think it will serve you well as a basic framework. I believe there is one significant and not entirely surprising item missing from the list. This is a desire to gain team skills. You may remember watching or being a little boy in early soccer matches. The aim of the game as interpreted by our little boy is to intercept the ball in his own team's goal mouth and then to dribble it like Juninho from one end of the pitch to the other and then to score. Massive applause! This unfortunately results in twenty little boys (the goal keeper's task is different and rather easier to understand) chasing the ball around the pitch.

The same anti-group activity may be seen in a care setting. What is missing here is team skills. Ideally I would have liked our subjects to have asked to learn to be better team players. I believe team skills are *absolutely* essential for effective therapeutic community participation. David Kennard has suggested in his discussion of the 'therapeutic community impulse' that a therapeutic community can only be created 'where those with a democratic tendency are sufficiently numerous' (Kennard 1991). I agree. In my opinion the most important democratic skill is graciously to lose an election and afterwards to support enthusiastically the winning majority.

Last of all I would suggest that you will gain and give most if you can learn how to be part of a living entity. Wrongly directed activity in a therapeutic community can poison or harm its process. The staff member needs to be self-critical, self-regulating, a good team member and unhesitatingly outspoken if he/she sees events or acts in the community which may harm its vitality.

WHAT ARE THE RESOURCES FOR EXPERIENCE, TRAINING AND LEARNING?

In the absence of a generally recognized training for therapeutic community work, you will need to collect a personal portfolio of experience, training and learning. The meaning of experience is self-evident. It is important, however, to make clear differentiation between training and learning. The former word implies passivity, the latter implies activity and self motivation. Initiative and creativity will be helpful attributes in a therapeutic community.

Both training and learning are important in a therapeutic community: training leads towards consistency of approach and conformity to certain standards of behaviour, learning leads towards individual autonomy and understanding. In practice, of course, we can 'learn' from a training course, and may get 'trained' in the process of learning. But the distinction is worth bearing in mind. In the following I indicate a number of potential resources for learning and training.

Working in a Therapeutic Community

Earlier I discussed reasons why this may not provide sufficient opportunities for learning by itself, but no training would make sense without it. The experience cannot be duplicated by books and lectures. How much learning does take place will depend, among other things, on the community's provision for supporting and training its new staff, on the staff member's own willingness to learn, and on the general level of morale and liveliness in the community at any particular time.

Given adequate morale in the community and openness in the new member certain kinds of learning are almost bound to occur. Stereotypes about mental illness and deviance will be broken down through participation with residents in everyday activities such as washing-up and gardening, and getting to know people as individuals rather than as types or diagnoses. The new member will learn some of the roles and techniques of the staff (although not necessarily understanding them), and will learn something about his or her own capacity for self-reliance, assertiveness, and tolerance of uncertainty.

Learning about oneself, especially about what are felt as one's inadequacies, may or may not be a constructive experience. A lot depends on what sort of support is available. Support may be provided in the regular staff feedback meetings, in a staff 'sensitivity' group, and through informal staff relationships. These are unlikely always to be enough and there is a risk that the newcomer's anxieties and frustrations will not be adequately explored if these are the only provisions available for doing so. Someone working in a therapeutic community for a month or so may not suffer too much from this – they may find it stimulating, revealing, and not too upsetting to their own stability. After leaving the community they can continue to digest and think about the experience. For those who stay longer, the experience may be too unsettling to learn from without additional sources of supervision and training.

Supervision

Supervision can take place either within the therapeutic community or outside it. Within the community one of the most useful aspects of supervision is the regular time and space it creates, set apart from the daily pressures and demands, to think about events and one's own part in them. The presence of the supervisor gives permission for such a period of detachment and reflection, which may otherwise be difficult to maintain in the middle of frequent requests for advice, information, help, and so forth.

A distinction should be made between two meanings which the term supervision can have in a therapeutic community. One refers to the situation in which someone is responsible for the work of a unit, or of a trainee, and oversees the work being done, giving advice, correcting mistakes, and so on. This kind of supervision has a place in the administrative aspects of therapeutic communities – writing reports, handling accounts, dealing with referrals. Within the sphere of psychotherapeutic activity, supervision has a different meaning. The supervisor helps the therapist to understand the relationships between events in the community, or in a particular group, taking into account the experience, feelings, attitudes, and so on, of all the participants. Particular attention is often given to the therapist's own responses. The supervisor leaves the responsibility for deciding how to respond to future events with the therapists. This contrasts with the former approach in which advice on the best procedure is given. In practice, the two forms of supervision may overlap a little but they are in principle doing different things. When people come together for supervision it may be important to clarify expectation about which sort of supervision is going to occur.

Various arrangements can be made for supervision. In my opinion supervision of a therapeutic community should be conducted in groups which mirror the structure of the community.

The position of the supervisor in relation to the rest of the community has important implications. Ideally he or she should have a good understanding of the way the community operates, but be sufficiently uninvolved in day-to-day events to be able to stand back and take an overview. The presence of an outside consultant has the advantage of bringing a fresh viewpoint to the community, but can also have disadvantages. He may be unaware of certain background issues affecting the staff, or be unable to judge the impact of his own contribution after he leaves. On the other hand, a staff member who is more in touch with underlying issues and able to judge the effects of his supervision may be blinkered by his commitment to seeing the community in a particular way. Where a supervisor is the director of the community or a senior staff member, difficulties may also arise from being seen as an authority figure within the community. How far this interferes with supervision will depend on various factors, one important one being whether the staff are also accountable to the supervisor for their work. Wherever possible it is better if supervision is not provided solely by the immediate superior in a professional hierarchy.

Peer Supervision

Outside the community, supervision can be arranged on a mutual, self-help basis. The Association of Therapeutic Communities fostered such a group for some years in the late 1970s and early 1980s (Keller and Roberts 1983). Staff from two or more therapeutic communities may form a group that meets regularly, taking it in turns to present an issue or problem that has occurred in one of their communities. In such a group the topics often concern recurring difficulties rather than immediate crises – for example, problems over staff leadership, attitudes towards sexual relationships between residents, reactions to violence or suicide. Both the writers participated in such a group and found it valuable. People who work in therapeutic communities understand each other's concerns very well. They can offer friendly, insightful, critical but constructive observations, in a relatively threat-free atmosphere, since turn by turn everyone is the learner and the supervisor. Given two or more communities within travelling distance of each other, the willingness to arrange periodic meetings and roughly equivalent levels of work experience, such a group has much to recommend it. In addition to being able to discuss one's own community, there is also a unique opportunity to learn how other communities function, in the kind of detail that would otherwise require one to work there oneself.

Visiting Other Communities

It doesn't really matter what another community is like – whether you agree with what they do, think they are better or worse than you are – seeing and hearing about another therapeutic community is useful. It raises questions, prompts new ideas, and provides the stimulus to think about the way you do things. Even if they work with a different type of resident or in a different setting, you will understand more about your own community from seeing how another works, and you may be able to establish useful links which can be developed for mutual learning and support. When visiting established, well-known communities it is worth bearing in mind that the image of a 'super-community', which has overcome all the problems you are struggling with will probably turn out to have been a mirage. When you get close, you realize that they are up against the same tensions, cliques, defensiveness and dissatisfactions that you thought you had left behind. Finding this out may reassure you that you are doing about as well as anyone else, and perhaps better than you thought.

Reading

Reading about the work is not a popular task for many therapeutic community staff. The work itself is often exhausting, and reading about it may seem like an additional burden. Yet reading something which helps you stand back from, and understand better, what it is you are involved in with a particular resident or situation, can actually help to make the work more bearable and interesting. As an aid to reading you can arrange informal 'study groups', where several people meet regularly to discuss articles or books they have read, or which one person has prepared comments on. The to and fro between a paper and the current life of your community is seldom dull.

Conferences, Workshops, etc.

Conferences and other meetings – lectures, workshops, symposia, seminars – come in all sizes and degrees of formality. Seminars and workshops are typically fairly small (ten to thirty people) and allow opportunities for discussion or active participation. Training workshops, taking place over a few days, are an invaluable introduction to the experiential aspect – the doing and the feeling – of working as a therapist. Conferences are typically for a large number of people, lasting anything from one day to a week. They often include social and fringe events that add to the interest of the more formal parts and are a good way to meet people with similar interests. In Britain the Association of Therapeutic Communities arranges a number of one-day conferences each year and an annual European conference – attended by staff from therapeutic communities in Holland, Italy, Greece, Germany and elsewhere – which takes place in Windsor each September.

Experiential Courses

An experiential course is one in which what you learn comes from the actual experience of taking part in the course, rather than from the information or opinions presented to you by speakers. The structure of an experiential course is different from a conference or lecture, although some courses combine the two kinds of learning. An experiential course is never fully structured in the sense that a lecture is fully structured – i.e. everyone knows exactly what they are supposed to do throughout a lecture. The time and the place are set, there may be certain guidelines and there will be one or more persons taking a training role of some kind. But the actual events that take place are left to the spontaneous actions of the participants. Faced with this situation people can and do react in a variety of ways: they may stay silent, try to find out what the 'trainer' wants, compete for leadership, agree to stick to safe topics, look for partners, and so on.

What is the point of this kind of experience? It helps you to learn about yourself, what sort of person you are, how you deal with people and situations when the rules don't tell you what to do. It enables you to see different therapeutic approaches and techniques as they happen and, more important, experience them from the patient's point of view.

You may also be able to practise taking the role of helper/therapist/leader if you want to. Some experiential courses are set up to demonstrate a particular therapeutic approach – for example psychodrama, group analysis, family therapy. Others offer a wider experience – for example therapeutic community living, working in groups. Some focus on a particular theme, such as resistance in therapy, authority and leadership, cultural differences. Some have as their aim simply the sharing of experience with others engaged in a similar work.

Whatever the stated aims or title, individuals attending an experiential course are likely to have different experiences and learn different things, so perhaps the stated aims should not be taken too much at face value. Much will depend on the personal styles of the staff running the course, and the expectations and readiness to learn of the individual participants. If you are lucky, the content and style of a course will fit with what you are ready to learn about yourself as a person and as a therapist, but it is hard to predict this in advance.

Experiential courses usually come in one of two lengths: a short, concentrated experience which takes place over a few consecutive days, and groups which meet regularly for a number of weeks or months. Short courses can create an intense emotional experience, in which people are by turns extremely anxious, happy, miserable, excited, and in which feelings of great warmth, intimacy and closeness can occur, as well as anger and distance. Some people find this overwhelming, others that it is of great benefit, others that it leaves them relatively untouched. One problem is that it is difficult to predict what your own experience will be, for the reasons mentioned above, and once the emotions have subsided there may be little long-term effect.

In following up people who attended one of the therapeutic community training weekends mentioned earlier, Kennard and Roberts (1980) found that a year later about half the participants responded to a questionnaire and were able to recall details of the event. Many of these reported small but significant changes in themselves, and a few had introduced some innovation into their work as a result of the course. The value of a short experiential course may, however, be as much in the break it provides, the opportunity for a shared experience which refreshes and reawakens interest and enthusiasm, as in the longer-term effects 'back home'.

Longer-term experiential courses allow time for the learning, and the putting into practice of what is learnt, to go at a slower pace. The experience is nearer to that of being a patient in therapy – in fact the line between them may be hard to draw except for the time available and the expectations of those involved. A weekly experiential group may lack the heady intensity of a short residential course, but allow for a more thorough and detailed exploration of individuals' experiences. It also provides more opportunity to experience and examine negative or ambivalent feelings. These are often overlooked or not fully acknowledged in short courses, which generate great cohesiveness and fellow feeling between participants.

Participating in an experiential group, whether short or long, provides an opportunity to share personal feelings and attitudes in a relatively accepting atmosphere. This effect is probably greatest when the members do not work together or have regular contact outside the group. When they do, issues of loyalty, confidentiality or accountability may increase resistance to free discussion. Such resistance is inevitable in groups consisting of the staff in one particular community, who may have relationships both in and out of work. However, the first task of such groups is usually to facilitate the work of the community rather than to provide the maximum opportunity for personal disclosure, and they cannot be regarded as the equivalent of belonging to a separate experiential group.

One further form of experiential learning of special value in therapeutic community work is to join a therapeutic community as a resident/client/patient member for a time. In this way, you live, work and feel alongside ordinary residents, without the distinction of being a student or the sense of it being a role-play. This approach to training is standard in some concept-based therapeutic communities for ex-addicts and is available in some psychotherapy training programmes such as those run by the Arbours Association in London and the Open Psychotherapeutic Centre in Athens, but is not generally available in hospital-based therapeutic communities. A simulated experience of being a resident in a therapeutic community is provided by the

Association of Therapeutic Communities as a short experiential course twice a year.

Personal Therapy and Training in Psychotherapy

There are several reasons why personal therapy can be of value. Some of these have already been mentioned. The impact of working in a therapeutic community may reawaken feelings of personal anxiety or unhappiness which need to be explored; and our interactions with patients or residents will be more sensitive and empathic if we have experienced for ourselves the pains and pleasures involved in personal therapy.

Whatever the professional motives for seeking therapy, it will only be of real value if there is a commitment to it for personal reasons. While any training requires some personal motivation, seeking therapy can only be a personal decision. Participating in experiential courses can give you some idea of what it will be like, to help you decide if it is what you want. If you do decide that you want to have therapy, what are the options?

One consideration to bear in mind is that you may have to pay for psychotherapy. Psychotherapists who work privately charge fees which may be high for students and low-paid staff, although some charge lower fees for people on lower incomes. If your organization employs psychotherapists you may be able to obtain psychotherapy without payment. Psychotherapists usually offer an initial session to discuss what you are looking for, and some offer a trial number of sessions. Do not be disheartened. Those who genuinely desire therapy will find a way of negotiating a manageable fee and paying it and value it all the more for not having had it for nothing!

A second consideration is whether to choose individual or group psychotherapy, and how frequent the sessions should be. Individual psychotherapy usually takes place once or twice a week but can be more frequent. Group therapy is usually weekly, sometimes twice weekly. If you are working in a therapeutic community and want to be able to relate your therapy to your work, group therapy will be more relevant. You will be able to appreciate directly the forces at work in a therapeutic group, and the presence of other patients in the group can help to break through the 'professional' way of thinking about problems that many mental health workers have. However, the choice of individual or group therapy is again a personal one, as well as being dependent on what is available, and both can be equally valuable. I would, however, quite strongly ask why, if you feel drawn to individual therapy, are you choosing therapeutic community work? Whichever therapy you choose you should think in terms of eighteen months or more, although individual psychotherapy focused on a particular problem can be shorter than this.

There is much to be gained from personal therapy. It will probably improve and enrich your life provided you do it because you really want to know and develop yourself. Undoubtedly it will enhance your work skills and prevent you from being destructive as well as diminishing the risk of your being psychologically damaged. But valuable as it is, in my opinion individual psychotherapy is almost entirely irrelevant *as a model* for therapeutic community work while group- analytic psychotherapy is only partially relevant. Therefore, if you wish to work in a therapeutic community, ideally you should be sure to:

(1)   Attend a number of experiential therapeutic community weekends.

(2)   Find a way of having a period of therapeutic community therapy.

(3)   Participate in an ongoing large or median group for at least twelve months.

MATCHING NEEDS AND RESOURCES

In the previous edition we produced what I now think was an over-elaborate chart to match need with resources. I will here attempt to indicate appropriate resources for your training without resorting to a chart.

I believe you can resort to the following for your training:

(1)   Yourself.

(2)   Your colleagues, managers and supervisors.

(3)   Your ever-growing experience of therapeutic community work.

(4)   A good library and librarian.

(5)   The Internet. I recommend you start your search with alta vista (http://www.altavista.com.) and take the opportunity offered to search on the European server, which will be faster and also seems to carry more Euro-relevant information.

(6)   The Association of Therapeutic Communities (ATC), tel: 0181-950 9557, email: Therap.Comm@btinternet.com.

In practice, the more resources you can utilize the better, as they will tend to enhance each other. For example, working in a therapeutic community simultaneously combined with supervision, a mutual supervision group with other staff, participating in an experiential group and occasional conferences and workshops, will create opportunities for learning in one situation that can be tried out in the others, which would not happen if you did one at a time.

You may be able to arrange some things yourself – for example, a seminar group for discussing books and articles, visits to other communities, meeting with staff from other communities. Other resources, such as supervision or experiential groups, tend to be more readily available in the larger cities where most psychotherapeutic work is carried out. However, it is worth contacting national training institutions and associations since they may have members in your area.

THE OUTCOME OF YOUR THERAPEUTIC COMMUNITY EDUCATION

I believe that a person who aspires to a career in therapeutic communities should have had an extensive education in the field. From all of this I hope you will have gained a clear idea of community and social processes as therapeutic agents. Also, you will gain a genuine secure and deeply felt knowledge of what a therapeutic community is. From this I would like you to have an allegiance to the therapeutic community as a living entity. I would like you to be a team player by choice. Finally I would wish you to have an intuitive feel for the complex patterns of relationship in community and social life. I would expect you to have struggled in your larger group experiences from hatred and fear of others to a genuine sense of Koinonia or fellowship. You will then be a natural democrat.

TOWARDS AN ACCREDITABLE TRAINING

I would like to outline a model of training which could be developed by a body such as the Association of Therapeutic Communities. This should be modelled on the accepted approach for a skills-based profession.

Selected students (self-selection is an important part of such a selection process) will have

(1)   experience of the method, initially as observer or participant observer.

(2)   personal therapy/personal development via the method in which training is sought.

(3)   theoretical understanding of the method.

(4)   supervised practice.

I believe that a monitoring/selecting/supervisory/qualifying body such as the Association of Therapeutic Communities could act to define a modular course (of which it could provide some modules and accredit the others) leading to various levels of achievement – foundation, intermediate, qualified.

The foundation level would enable somebody to demonstrate their desire and aptitude for ongoing work in a therapeutic community. At the intermediate level the trainee is in the middle of a therapeutic community career and could be viewed as capable of sharing with others the task of providing a therapeutic community process. The qualified person would have reached a level at which an employer could view him as worth considering as a therapeutic community manager, as a consultant to one or more therapeutic communities, as a possible change agent or as capable of developing and supervising a therapeutic community research project.

Thus I see a great deal of scope for individual initiative in the acquisition of a portfolio of modules. For certification/qualification there will be an unavoidable need to have all the right modules and an ability to apply learning in practice.

Professional Institute versus University Degree or Diploma

There is a tendency at present for universities to adopt training courses in the psychotherapies. It is increasingly possible to obtain graduate and postgraduate degrees in psychotherapy and counselling. This is fine for the theoretical element of training. However, I would like to re-emphasize that a degree is not a qualification. Universities have *traditionally* never aspired to train people in professional skills and there is a long tradition of separate non-academic bodies granting a licence to practise. Usually following some form of apprenticeship. This has been and is the case for barristers, doctors and bricklayers. Thus while I see no problem with university involvement (and indeed welcome it) it will remain the duty of an evaluation body concerned with practice skills, safety and ethics to oversee the part of the course which teaches and examines these skills.

The Association of Therapeutic Communities/Royal College of Nursing Initiative

From 1986 to 1992 there was an annual one-year module of teaching of therapeutic community practice with a substantial experiential component, including a simulated therapeutic community. This was initially designed by a mixed Royal College of Nursing/Association of Therapeutic Communities committee and was quite successful for a few years. Although intended to be multidisciplinary it largely attracted nurses. Some participants appear to have gained a great deal but eventually there was a loss of momentum and the module was abandoned because of lack of demand.

CONCLUDING REMARKS

(1)   There is now considerable scope for a renewed demand form purchasers for a range of effective therapeutic communities tailored for client requirements.

(2)   This demand may exceed the ability of currently active therapeutic communities to provide suitable staff unless training is developed quite rapidly.

(3)   There is a strong possibility of developments which will enable you to envisage an enduring career as a therapeutic community therapist or manager.

(4)   If the above assumptions are correct it will be important for the new wave of therapeutic communities to have trained people with a real knowledge of therapeutic communities and a capacity to nurture them.

(5)   I believe that the Association of Therapeutic Communities should heighten its awareness of the probability of a huge increase in demand for therapeutic communities. It should take charge of setting standards and requirements of what would seem to me to be a naturally shaped three-tiered climb to accreditable qualification (see above).

I would like to end this chapter by commenting on how the development of the therapeutic community has always been subject to tidal processes in societal development, which themselves are an expression of the yin to yang to yin phenomenon. Each time the tide comes in I believe we gain a little more clarity about the therapeutic community and ways in which it can be most effectively applied. In my opinion the high points of the tide have been the development of democracy in Athens, Tuke's work at The Retreat, Stack Sullivan at Chestnut Lodge, Foulkes at Northfield, Maxwell Jones at the Henderson and David Clark at Fulbourn. The next high point may be in your hands!

PART III

Further information

This section is designed to help you if you are:

- doing a project and need more in-depth information or ideas
- wanting to get some first-hand experience by visiting a therapeutic community
- looking for training in therapeutic community practice and ideas
- seeking contact with others with a similar professional background or interests
- wanting to develop the setting you are working in towards a therapeutic community way of working.

KEY PROFESSIONAL ORGANIZATIONS IN
THE UNITED KINGDOM

Association of Therapeutic Communities (ATC)

Founded in 1972, this is the main organization in the United Kingdom supporting the development of therapeutic communities across the different sectors and services: in the health service, social services, prison service and the voluntary sector. The ATC arranges conferences with different host therapeutic communities, an annual European conference each September and training events including its well-known 'simulated therapeutic community' weekends. There are special interest groups for members concerned with training, research, and therapeutic communities in specialist settings such as prisons. The ATC does not operate a referral service but publishes a directory of therapeutic communities and can provide contacts and access to specialist advice. The ATC publishes the quarterly journal *Therapeutic Communities* and a quarterly Newsletter. For further information and individual and institutional membership rates contact the Administrator.

Association of Therapeutic Communities
13–15 Pine Street
London, EC1R 0JH
UK
(+44) 0181-950 9557

Therap.Comm@btinternet.com.
See the ATC website at http://psyctc.sghms.ac.uk/atc/wshopost.htm

Planned Environment Therapy Trust

'A home for research and discussion about therapeutic community.' This is a relatively small charitable trust founded in 1966 to promote research and discussion furthering the support and use of approaches to living and working with unhappy, disturbed, delinquent or disturbing individuals, in which all the resources of a thoughtfully created environment, the shared living experience, and above all the enormous healing potential of relationships, are brought together for therapeutic ends. The specific objects of the Trust, to quote from the original title deed, are: 'To investigate and study, publish results and expositions and train workers and carry out in practice methods of treatment of emotionally disturbed, maladjusted or delinquent children, young persons or adults, by means of a Planned Environment Therapy especially in association with specialist psycho-therapy.'

The Planned Environment Therapy Trust Archive was founded in 1989 in order to gather and protect the papers of individuals, institutions and organizations involved in environment therapy/milieu therapy/therapeutic community, and in that 'democratic' or 'alternative' approach to schools and education which has been called 'therapeutic communities for normal children'. The Archive forms the core of the Study Centre, which includes the library, seminar rooms, and living accommodation for visiting students and scholars. The Study Centre has the broader aim of encouraging and promoting research and discussion in the fields covered by the Archive. It does this in part through an active oral history recording programme; through small grants; through publication; and through exhibitions, meetings, seminars and small conferences.

Planned Environment Therapy Trust Archive and Study Centre
Church Lane
Toddington
Cheltenham
Glos. GL54 5DQ
UK
(+44) 01242-62 01 25

archive@pettarchiv.org.uk.
See the PETT website at http://www.pettarchiv.org.uk

Charterhouse Group
Formed in 1987, the Charterhouse Group is an association formed by the directors of a number of therapeutic communities for children and young people. The broad aim of the Group is to support and promote high quality care, education and treatment for emotionally disturbed children and young people based on psychodynamic principles. The Group provides a programme of activities and training for staff, organizes national conferences and meetings of focused work groups. It also offers information on individual therapeutic communities to professionals seeking to place a child or young person.

The Charterhouse Group
150 Waterloo Road
London, SE1 8SB
UK
Tel: (+44) 0171-803 0550;
Fax: (+44) 0171-261 1307

Standing Conference on Drug Abuse
The Standing Conference on Drug Abuse (SCODA) seeks to reduce the harmful effects of drug use through informed debate, and through the promotion of best practice and effective, comprehensive services. It is an independent membership organization, providing a voice for drug services and others concerned about the effects of drug use on individuals and communities. Specific projects include a professional enquiry service, a sponsorship and

funding advisory service, developing standards for a range of specific drug and alcohol interventions and a European liason service providing information on European funding opportunities and putting UK services in touch with European partners.

Publications include *Residential Drug Services: A Comprehensive Guide to Rehabilitation in England and Wales*. This is a directory designed to help individuals, referrers and purchasers find services which best meet their needs. Residential services are grouped into the following categories: Christian philosophy; Christian staff; General; Minnesota Model; Modified Minnesota Model; and Therapeutic Community. It is priced at £20/£16 to SCODA members.

SCODA
Waterbridge House
32–36 Loman Street
London SE1 0FE
UK
Tel: 0171-928 9500
Fax: 0171-928 3343

See the SCODA website at http://www.ncvo-vol.org.uk/scoda.html

United Kingdom Council for Psychotherapy (UKCP)

The voluntary registration system for psychotherapists in Britain is currently the province of the UKCP although there is a 'confederacy' of psychoanalytic institutions (BCP) who have split off from the UKCP. The UKCP works by registering training organizations which then recommend that trainees are (or are not) registerable by the UKCP itself. The UKCP requires that training organizations have formal codes of ethics and practice and will strike people off the register for failing to live up to these. In 1998 there is as yet no UKCP-registered training specifically for therapeutic communities, although some member organizations do provide relevant experience.

UKCP
167–169 Great Portland Street
London, WC1N 5FB
UK
Tel: (+44) 0171-436 3002
Fax: 0171-436 3013

Society for Psychotherapy Research

The Society for Psychotherapy Research (SPR) is an international, interdisciplinary organization dedicated to the scientific study of psychotherapy in all of its various forms. There are currently four regional chapters (North America,

South America, Europe, United Kingdom) and over one thousand members worldwide. The organization meets annually to exchange information among psychotherapy researchers from around the world. The UK chapter also hosts its own annual three-day conference each spring, and includes a number of members who work and carry out research in therapeutic communities.

SPR Administrator
1 Ansley Grove
Heaton Moor
Stockport SK4 3LF
UK
Tel/Fax: (+44) 0161-432 4507

See the SPR website at http://psyctc.sghms.ac.uk/spruk/

THERAPEUTIC COMMUNITIES IN THE UNITED KINGDOM

The following are some of the well-established therapeutic communities in different sectors in England mentioned in the book. Most therapeutic communities are willing to accept visitors by prior arrangement (but not without notice). Some accept visitors for a day, others prefer longer. Some communities provide staff training programmes.

Adults – NHS

Cassel Hospital
1 Ham Common
Richmond
Surrey TW10 7JF
Tel: (+44) 0181-940 8181

Henderson Hospital
2 Homeland Drive
Sutton
Surrey SM2 5LT
Tel: (+44) 0181-661 1611

Winterbourne House (Day therapeutic community)
53–55 Argyle Road
Reading
Berks. RG1 7YL
Tel: (+44) 01734-561250

Adult – Alternative Asylum

The Arbours Communities and Training Programme
6 Church Lane
London N8 7BU

Tel: (Communities) 0181-340 7646
(Training) 0181-341 0196

Philadelphia Association
4 Marty's Yard
17 Hampstead High Street
London NW3 1QW
Tel: 0171-794 2652

Adult Offenders

HMP (Her Majesty's Prison) Grendon Underwood
Aylesbury
Bucks HPl8 OTL
Tel: (+44) 01296-770301

Drug Rehabilitation

Ley Community
Sandy Croft
Sandy Lane
Yarnton
Oxon OX5 1PB
Tel: 01865-371777

Children and Adolescents

Contact:
The Charterhouse Group
150 Waterloo Road
London SE1 8SB
Tel: (+44) 0171-261 1307

REST OF THE WORLD CONTACTS
FOR FURTHER INFORMATION

Australia

Dr Peter Bott
PO Box 1808
Chatswood
New South Wales 2057

Denmark

Hans Kornerup
cand.psych.
Nebs Mollevej 90
DK–4174
Jystrup Midtsjaelland

Finland

Professor Matti Isohanni
Department of Psychiatry
University of Oulu
Peltolantie 5
FIN–90220 Oulu

Germany

Professor Dr Martin Teising
Arzt für Psychiatrie, Psychotherapie, Psychoanalyse
Ludwig-Braun-Straße 13
36251 Bad Hersfeld

Greece

Dr Ioannis K. Tsegos
Open Psychotherapeutic Centre
S Haralambi 1 & Mavromihali 114
72 Athens

Israel

Professor Stanley Schneider
PO Box 8428
Jerusalem

Italy

Dr Enrico Pedriali
Largo Settimio Severo 3
20144 Milano

Netherlands

Jan Hartman
Van Lenneplaan 4
1985 AG Driehuis

Norway

Professor Sigmund Karterud
Department of Psychiatry
Ullevål University Hospital
N-0407 Oslo

Slovenia

Professor Milos Kobal
UKC – Univerzitetna Psichiatricna Klinika
Center Za Mentalno Zdravje
61105 Ljubljana
Poljanski Nasip 58

Sweden

Dr Goran Ahlin
Director, Institute of Psychotherapeutic Psychotherapy
Långbro S-125 85 Älvsjö

United States

Professor Rudolf Moos
Center for Health Care Evaluation
Department of Psychiatry TD-114
Stanford University
Stanford
California

The following international organizations are concerned with the treatment and rehabilitation of drug abusers using the concept-based methods described in Chapter 7.

World Federation of Therapeutic Communities

Founded in 1980, the World Federation of Therapeutic Communities (WFTC) states as its purpose, 'to join together in a world wide association of sharing, understanding and cooperation within the global TC Movement, as well as to widen recognition and acceptance of the Therapeutic Community and the Therapeutic Community approach among health organizations and health delivery systems of international and national bodies.' WFTC calls for a 'holistic approach to the healing of human beings, drawing on the helping services from non-degreed, ex-users to degreed professionals from the full spectrum of helping disciplines.' There are three regional federations in Europe, Asia and South America.

World Federation of Therapeutic Communities
54 West 40th Street
New York
New York 10018, USA
Tel: (212) 354-6000
Fax: (212) 921-8901

European Federation of Therapeutic Communities
Phoenix House Haga
1850 Mysen, Norway
Tel: 47-6-9891133
Fax: 47-6-9893265

Asian Federation of Therapeutic Communities
257 Mahidol Bldg
Rajvithi Road
Bangkok 10400
Thailand
Tel: (622) 245-5522
Fax: (662) 248-1722

Federacion LatinoAmericana de Comunidades Terapeuticas
Calle 57, 43–20
A.A. 8558
Medellin
Colombia
Tel: (94) 284-4304
Fax: (94) 254-9902

Therapeutic Communities of America

As the national organization of drug-free, self-help substance-abuse treatment
and rehabilitation agencies, Therapeutic Communities of America (TCA) provides a platform for the discussion of substance abuse policy, legislation and
service issues. It serves in a pivotal leadership role in Washington DC and
speaks to regional, national and world forums on behalf of its constituency.
Founded in 1975, TCA has grown to a consortium of over four hundred programmes throughout the United States and Canada.

Therapeutic Communities of America National Office
1611 Connecticut Avenue NW Suite 4-B
Washington, DC, 20009
USA
Tel: (202) 296-3503
Fax: (202) 518-5475

Recommended Reading

There is an enormous amount of literature available. Below is a 'bench' collection of books: classics and some of the best recent publications. The Association of Therapeutic Communities provides recommended reading lists of articles in the areas of development and principles, different client groups, outcome research and recent publications. It also published a comprehensive bibliography of papers appearing in the quarterly journal *Therapeutic Communities*, divided into relevant categories.

Ten Books for Further Reading

Rapoport, Robert (1960) *Community as Doctor.* London: Tavistock.

Jones, Maxwell (1968) *Social Psychiatry in Practice.* Harmondsworth: Pelican.

Bridgeland, Maurice (1971) *Pioneer Work with Maladjusted Children: A Study in the Development of Therapeutic Education.* London: Staples Press.

Sugarman, Barry (1974) *Daytop Village: A Therapeutic Community.* New York: Holt, Rinehart and Winston.

Berke, Joseph (1979) *I Haven't Had to Go Mad Here.* Harmondsworth: Penguin.

Hinshelwood, R.D. and Manning, Nick (1979) *Therapeutic Communities: Reflections and Progress.* London: Routledge.

Hinshelwood R.D. (1987) *What Happens in Groups.* London: Free Association Books.

Manning, Nick (1989) *The Therapeutic Community Movement: Charisma and Routinization.* London: Routledge.

Clark, David (1996) *The Story of a Mental Hospital: Fulbourn 1853–1983.* London: Process Press.

Cullen, Eric, Jones, Lawrence and Woodward, Roland (1997) *Therapeutic Communities for Offenders.* London: Wiley.

Therapeutic Communities – The International Journal for Therapeutic and Supportive Organizations

The Journal of the Association of Therapeutic Communities, published quarterly and available by direct subscription or with membership of the Association.

The Journal takes a positive and lively approach to developing awareness of the psychodynamics of what happens across a wide range of social and professional contexts. This takes in many levels of human experience, from the intrapsychic and interpersonal to the group or team, to the organization as a whole and the wider socio-political system. A particular feature is the

Journal's concern with the relationship between individual experience, collective responsibility and issues of empowerment.

Journal Administrator
Association of Therapeutic Communities,
13–15 Pine Street
London EC1R 0JH, UK
Tel/Fax: (+44) 0181-950 9557

email Therap.Comm@btinternet.com

References

Almond, R. (1974) *The Healing Community*. New York: Jason Aronson.

Antze, P. (1979) 'The role of ideologies in peer psychotherapy groups.' In H. Lieberman and L.D. Borman *Self-help Groups for Coping with Crisis*. London: Jossey-Bass.

Barker, P. and Davidson, B. (eds) (1996) *Psychiatric Nursing: Ethical Strife*. London: Edward Arnold.

Barnes, E. (ed) (1968) *Psychosocial Nursing: Studies from the Cassel Hospital*. London: Tavistock.

Barnes, E., Griffiths, P., Ord, J. and Wells, D. (eds) (1998) *Face to Face with Distress*. Oxford: Butterworth-Heinemann.

Barnes, M. and Berke, J. (1971) *Mary Barnes: Two Accounts of a Journey Through Madness*. London: Hart-Davis MacGibbon.

Barton, R. (1959) *Institutional Neurosis*. Bristol: Wright.

Berke, J. (1979) *I Haven't Had to Go Mad Here*. Harmondsworth: Penguin.

Berke, J. (1980) 'Kingsley Hall.' In E. Jansen (ed) *The Therapeutic Community*. London: Croom Helm.

Berke, J., Masoliver, C. and Ryan, T. (eds) (1995) *Sanctuary*. London: Process Press.

Bessin, A. (1977) 'The miracle of the therapeutic community: From birth to post-partum insanity to full recovery.' In *Proceedings of The 2nd World Conference of Therapeutic Communities*. Montreal: Portage Press.

Bion, W.R. (1946) 'The leaderless group project.' *Bulletin of the Menninger Clinic 10*, 77–81.

Bion, W.R. (1961) *Experiences in Groups*. London: Tavistock.

Blake, R., Millard, D.W. and Roberts, J.P. (1984) 'Therapeutic community principles in an integrated local authority community mental health service.' *International Journal of Therapeutic Communities 5*, 4, 243–273.

Bloom, S. (1997) *Creating Sanctuary*. London: Routledge.

Bockoven, J.S. (1956) 'Moral Treatment in American Society.' *Journal of Nervous and Mental Diseases 124*, 167–94.

Boyle, M. (1990) *Schizophrenia: A Scientific Delusion?* London: Fontana.

Boyle, M. (1996) 'Schizophrenia: the fallacy of diagnosis.' *Changes 14*, 1, 5–13.

Bridgeland, M. (1971) *Pioneer Work with Maladjusted Children*. London: Staples Press.

Briggs, D. (1972) 'A transitional therapeutic community in prison.' In J.S. Whiteley, D. Briggs and N. Turner (eds) *Dealing with Deviants*. London: Hogarth Press.

Brown, D. and Pedder, J. (1991) *Introduction to Psychotherapy: An Outline of Psychodynamic Principles and Practice 2nd edition*. London: Tavistock.

Burridge, T. (1997) 'On joining a therapeutic community.' *Therapeutic Communities 18*, 2, 145–147.

Caltagirone, I. and Smargiassi, M. (1997) 'Therapeutic and non-therapeutic communities.' *Therapeutic Communities 18*, 3, 167–181.

Campbell, P. (1996) 'The history of the user movement in the United Kingdom.' In T. Heller, J. Reynolds, R. Gomm, R. Muston and S. Pattison (eds) *Mental Health Matters: A Reader.* Basingstoke: Macmillan.

Campling, P. (1992) 'Audit of premature departure in a therapeutic community – a preliminary report.' *Therapeutic Communities 13*, 1, 45–53.

Caudill, W.A. (1958) *The Psychiatric Hospital as a Small Society.* Cambridge, Mass.: Harvard University Press.

Chiesa, M. (1997) 'A combined in-patient/out-patient programme for severe personality disorders.' *Therapeutic Communities 18*, 4, 297–309.

Clark, D.H. (1964) *Administrative Therapy.* London: Tavistock.

Clark, D.H. (1965) 'The therapeutic community – concept, practice and future.' *British Journal of Psychiatry 111*, 947–54.

Clark, D.H. (1977) 'The therapeutic community.' *British Journal of Psychiatry 131*,. 553–64.

Clark, D.H. (1996) *The Story of a Mental Hospital: Fulbourn 1853–1983.* London: Process Books.

Clark, D.H. (1997) In discussion with David Kennard. Toddington: PETT Archive.

Cooper, D. (1967) *Psychiatry and Anti-Psychiatry.* London: Tavistock.

Cox, J. (1998) 'Reflections on contemporary community psychiatry: Where is the therapy?' *Therapeutic Communities 19*, 1, 3–10.

Croese, N. (1997) 'Too close to home.' *Therapeutic Communities 18*, 3, 195–207.

Croft, S. and Beresford, P. (1997) 'User views.' *Changes 15*, 2, 158–9.

Cullen, E. (1994) 'Grendon: The therapeutic prison that works.' *Therapeutic Communities 15*, 4, 301–311.

Cullen, E. (1997) 'Can a prison be a therapeutic community? The Grendon template.' In E. Cullen, L. Jones and R. Woodward (eds) *Therapeutic Communities for Offenders.* New York: Wiley.

Cullen, E., Jones, L. and Woodward, R. (eds) (1997) *Therapeutic Communities for Offenders.* New York: Wiley.

De Leon, G. (1994) 'The therapeutic community: Toward a general theory and model.' In F.M. Timms, G. De Leon and N. Jainchill (eds) *Therapeutic Community: Advances in Research and Application.* Rockville: National Institute on Drug Abuse.

Dolan, B.M., Warren, F.M., Menzies, D. and Norton, K. (1996) 'Cost-offset following specialist treatment of severe personality disorders.' *Psychiatric Bulletin 20*, 413–417.

Fees, C. (1995) 'The Planned Environment Therapy Trust Archive and Study Centre.' *Therapeutic Communities 16*, 1, 73–75.

Foulkes, S.R. (1948) *Introduction to Group-Analytic Psychotherapy.* London: Heinemann.

Foulkes, S.R. (1964) *Therapeutic Group Analysis.* London: George Allen & Unwin.

Frank, J. (1979) 'What is psychotherapy?' In S. Block (ed) *An Introduction to the Psychotherapies.* Oxford University Press.

Freeman, H. (ed) (1965) *Psychiatric Hospital Care.* London: Baillere, Tindall & Cassell.

Glaser, F. (1977) 'The origins of the drug-free therapeutic community – a retrospective history.' In P. Vamos and J.E. Brown (eds) *Proceedings of The 2nd World Conference of Therapeutic Communities.* Montreal: Portage Press.

Goffman, E. (1961) *Asylums.* New York: Doubleday. Republished (1968), Harmondsworth: Penguin.

Greenwood, J., Ibanez, J. and Rose, S. (1994) 'Personal reflections on being a resident therapist.' *Therapeutic Communities 15,* 1, 55–63.

Gunn, J. *et al.* (1978) *Psychiatric Aspects of Imprisonment.* London: Academic Press.

Harrison, T. and Clarke, D. (1992) 'The Northfield Experiments.' *British Journal of Psychiatry 160,* 698–708.

Higgins, B. (1997) 'Does anyone feel they need support tonight?' *Therapeutic Communities 18,* 1, 55–61.

Hinshelwood, R.D. (1980) 'The seeds of disaster.' *International Journal of Therapeutic Communities 1,* 3, 181–8.

Hinshelwood, R.D. (1987) *What Happens in Groups.* London: Free Association Books.

Hinshelwood, R.D. (1996) 'Communities and their health.' *Therapeutic Communities 17,* 3, 173–182.

Hinshelwood, R.D. (1997) 'I have an idea.' In D. Kennard and N. Small (eds) *Living Together.* London: Quartet.

Hobson, R.F. (1979) 'The messianic community.' In R.D. Hinshelwood and N. Mannings (eds) *Therapeutic Communities – Reflections and Progress.* London: Routledge & Kegan Paul.

Ingleby, D. (ed) (1981) *Critical Psychiatry.* Harmondsworth: Penguin.

Irwin, F. (1995) 'The therapeutic ingredients of baking a cake.' *Therapeutic Communities 16,* 4, 263–68.

Isohanni, M. (1993) 'The therapeutic community movement in Finland – past, current and future views.' *Therapeutic Communities 14,* 2, 81–90.

Jansen, E. (1980) 'Therapeutic community models: IV. The Richmond Fellowship.' In E. Jansen (ed) *The Therapeutic Community.* London: Croom Helm.

Johnstone, L. (1989) *Users and Abusers of Psychiatry.* London: Routledge.

Jones, K. (1996) Moral Treatment in Perspective. Paper presented at the bicentennial conference held at The Retreat, York, October 1996.

Jones, M. (1968) *Social Psychiatry in Practice.* Harmondsworth: Penguin.

Jones, M. (1979) 'The therapeutic community, social learning and social change.' In R.D. Hinshelwood and N. Manning (eds) *Therapeutic Community – Reflections and Progress.* London: Routledge & Kegan Paul.

Jones, M. (1982) *The Process of Change.* London: Routledge.

Keller, A. and Roberts, J.P. (1983) 'The ATC supervisors group: an experiment in the supervision of therapeutic communities.' *International Journal of Therapeutic Communities 4*, 1, 13–21.

Kennard, D. (1991) 'The therapeutic community impulse: A recurring democratic tendency in troubled times.' *Changes 9*, 1, 33–43.

Kennard, D. (1994) 'The future revisted: New frontiers for therapeutic communities.' *Therapeutic Communities 15*, 2, 107–113.

Kennard, D. and Roberts, J.P. (1978) 'Learning from experience in a therapeutic community.' *Group Analysis X1*, 3, 223–226.

Kennard, D. and Roberts, J.P. (1980) 'Therapeutic community training: A one year follow-up.' *Group Analysis XIII, 1, 54–56.*

Kennard, D. and Roberts, J.P. (1983) 'Questions of Training.' In D. Kennard *An Introduction to Therapeutic Communities.* London: Routledge.

Kjartansdottir, S. (1994) 'A community in crisis – A view from the kitchen.' *Therapeutic Communities 15*, 2, 125–132.

Knowles, J. (1992) 'Audit for therapeutic communities.' *Therapeutic Communities 13*, 1, 55–56.

Knowles, J. (1995) 'Therapeutic communities in today's world.' *Therapeutic Communities 16*, 2, 97–102.

Kotowicz, Z. (1997) *R.D. Laing and the Paths of Anti-psychiatry.* London: Routledge.

Laing, R.D. (1967) *The Politics of Experience.* Harmondsworth: Penguin.

Laing, R.D. (1971) *The Politics of the Family and Other Essays.* London: Tavistock.

Leff, J. (ed) (1997) *Care in the Community: Illusion or Reality?* New York: Wiley.

Lieberman, N., Borman, L. and Associates (1979) *Self-help Groups for Coping with Crisis.* London: Jossey-Bass.

Linehan, M. (1993) *Cognitive Behavioural Treatment of Borderline Personality Disorders.* London: Guildford Press.

Lipton, D. (1997) *Therapeutic Community Treatment Programming for Drug Abusers in Corrections.* New York: National Development and Research Institute.

McAlpin, S. (1996) 'Progressing towards separation.' *Therapeutic Communities 17*, 3, 193–203.

McGlashen, T.H. and Levy, S.T. (1977) 'Sealing-over in a therapeutic community.' *psychiatry 40*, 55–65.

Mahony, N. (1979) 'My stay at the henderson therapeutic community.' In R.D. Hinshelwood and N. Manning *Therapeutic Communities: Reflections and Progress.* London: Routledge & Kegan Paul.

Main, T. (1946) 'The hospital as a therapeutic institution.' *Bulletin of the Menninger Clinic 10*, 66–70.

Main, T. (1975) 'Some psychodynamics of large groups.' In L. Kreeger (ed) *The Large Group.* London: Constable.

Main, T. (1977) The concept of the therapeutic community: Variations and vicissitudes, S.H. Foulkes annual lecture, published as special supplement to *Group Analysis 10*, 2.

Manning, N.P. (1976) 'What happened to the therapeutic community?' In K. Jones and S. Baldwin (eds) *Yearbook of Social Policy 1975*. London: Routledge and Kegan Paul.

Mandelbrote, B.M. (1965) 'The use of psychodynamic and sociodynamic principles in the treatment of psychotics.' *Comprehensive Psychiatry 6*, 6, 381–7.

Markezinis, M., Protopapa, A. and Papageorgiou, P. (1992) 'A model therapeutic community for patients with rotating shifts.' Paper presented at Annual Windsor Conference, Windsor, September 1992.

Martin, D. (1962) *Adventure in Psychiatry*. London: Cassirer.

Masson, J. (1989) *Against Therapy*. London: Harper Collins.

Matilda (1994) 'Confessions of a misfit.' *Therapeutic Communities 15*, 2, 115–124.

Meinrath, M. and Roberts, J. (1982) 'On being a good enough staff member.' *International Journal of Therapeutic Communities 3*, 1, 7–14.

Millard, D. (1993) 'The Minister at Grendon.' *Therapeutic Communities 14*, 1, 11–18.

Moore, B. (1998) 'In-service training at Threshold: A therapeutic community organization in Northern Ireland.' *Therapeutic Communities 19*, 1, 57–66.

Mosher, L.R., Mann, A. and Matthews, S.M. (1975) 'Soteria: Evaluation of a homebased treatment for schizophrenia.' *American Journal of Orthopsychiatry 45*, 455–67.

Mosher, L.R. and Burti, L. (1994) *Community Mental Health: A Practical Guide*. New York: W.W. Norton.

Orbach, S. (1994) *What's really Going on Here?* London: Virago.

Parry-Jones, W. (1981) 'The model of the Geel Lunatic Colony and its influence on the nineteenth century asylum system in Britain.' In A. Scull (ed) *Madness, Mad Doctors and Madmen*. London: Athlene Press.

Pedriali, E. (1997) 'Italian therapeutic communities: From historical analysis to hypotheses for change.' *Therapeutic Communities 18*, 1, 3–13.

Pines, M. (1983) 'The contribution of S.H. Foulkes to group therapy.' In M. Pines (ed) *The Evolution of Group Analysis*. London: Routledge.

Porter, R. (1996) Foreword to *The Story of a Mental Hospital* by David Clark. London: Process Books.

Pullen, G.P. (1982) 'Street: The seventeen day community.' *International Journal of Therapeutic Communities 2*, 2, 115–126.

Rapoport, R.N. (1960) *Community as Doctor*. London: Tavistock.

Read, J. and Reynolds, J. (1996) *Speaking our minds: An anthology of personal experiences of mental distress and its consequences*. London: MIND.

Reed, J. (1994) 'A review of services for mentally disordered offenders and others with similar needs: Report of the sub-committee on psychopathic disorder.' department of health/home office.

Riesman, D. (1969) *The Lonely Crowd.* New York: Yale University Press.

Roberts, J.P. (1982) 'Destructive processes in a therapeutic community.' *International Journal of Therapeutic Communities 1,* 3, 159–170.

Rothman, D. (1971) *The Discovery of the Asylum.* Boston: Little, Brown.

Rowe, D. (1995) *Dorothy Rowe's Guide to Life.* London: Harper-Row.

Schatzman, M. (1969) 'Madness and morals.' In J. Berke (ed) *Counter Culture.* London: Peter Owen. Reprinted in R. Boyers and R. Orrill (eds) (1972) *Laing and Anti-Psychiatry.* Harmondsworth: Penguin.

Scull, A. (1979) *Museums of Madness.* London: Allen Lane.

Smail, D. (1988) *Taking Care: An Alternative to Therapy.* London: Dent.

Smith, M. (1981) 'Working my ticket.' *International Journal of Therapeutic Communities 2,* 1, 43–51.

Stanton, A. and Schwartz, H. (1954) *The Mental Hospital.* New York: Basic Books.

Sugarman, B. (1968) The Phoenix Unit: Alliance against illness. *New Society.* London: New Science Publications.

Sugarman, B. (1974) *Daytop Village – A Therapeutic Community.* New York: Holt, Rinehart & Winston.

Taggart, J. (1993) 'Reflections on a summer placement.' *Therapeutic Communities 14,* 2, 119–125.

Tsegos, I.K. (1982) A psychotherapeutic community in Athens. Paper presented at Annual Windsor Conference, Windsor, September.

Tsegos, I. (1996) 'Fifty years of an amateur enthusiasm (On the avoidance of training and of professional identity in therapeutic community).' *Therapeutic Communities 17,* 3, 159–165.

Tucker, S. (1998) 'Dialogue: Training for active citizenship.' *Therapeutic Communities 19,* 1, 41–53.

Tuke, S. (1813) *Description of The Retreat.* Republished in 1996, London: Process Books.

Vanier, J. (1982) *The Challenge of L'Arche.* London: Darton, Longman and Todd.

Wallenberg Pachaly, A. von (1992) 'The Time-Limited Psychoanalytic Milieutherapeutic Community.' *Therapeutic Communities 13,* 4, 193–207.

Wallenberg Pachaly, A.V. (1997) 'The large group and the large group system.' *Therapeutic Communities 18,* 3, 223–239.

Weatherill, R. (1997) 'Smooth operators.' In D. Kennard and N. Small (eds) *Living Together.* London: Quartet.

Wexler, H. (1997) 'Therapeutic communities in American prisons.' In E. Cullen, L. Jones and R. Woodward (eds) *Therapeutic Communities for Offenders.* New York: Wiley.

Whiteley, J.S. (1980) 'The Henderson Hospital.' *International Journal of Therapeutic Communities 1,* 1, 38–58.

Whiteley, J.S. and Collis, M. (1987) 'The Therapeutic factors in group psychotherapy applied to the therapeutic community.' *International Journal of Therapeutic Communities 1*, 21–32.

Wills, W.D. (1971) *Spare the Child: The Story of an Experimental Approved School.* Harmondsworth: Penguin.

Wilmer, H. (1958) *Social Psychiatry in Action.* Springfield: Charles C. Thomas.

Yablonsky, L. (1965) *Synanon: The Tunnel Back.* New York: Macmillan.

Yalom, I. (1985) *The Theory and Practice of Group Psychotherapy.* New York: Basic Books.

Subject Index

Author Index